the Bible Detective

MIXED-UP STORIES TO TEST YOUR BIBLE KNOWLEDGE

CAROL SMITH

BARBOUR
PUBLISHING, INC.
Uhrichsville, Ohio

© 2000 by The Livingstone Corporation.

ISBN 1-57748-838-5

Developed by The Livingstone Corporation.

Special thanks to Roddy Smith, Ashley Jones, and Ann Marie Clark
for their contributions.

Published by Barbour Publishing, Inc., P.O. Box 719, Uhrichsville,
Ohio 44683 http://www.barbourbooks.com

 Member of the
Evangelical Christian
Publishers Association

Printed in the United States of America.

Contents

INTRODUCTION

We often feel familiar with the truth—until we're faced with a half-truth and have to separate fact from fiction. That's what the stories in *The Bible Detective* are about. While each one contains a good dose of biblical truth, based on an account that you've probably heard in Sunday school, each story also includes a measure of fiction that will test your wits.

It's up to you to find the errors. Sometimes the most obvious are the most difficult to catch. For each story, the Scripture passage is listed so you can check the facts yourself. And, of course, you can also read the solution, provided at the end of the book.

Start with the easiest ones and then "ease" yourself up to the most difficult. To keep within the biblical time period, the level of difficulty is indicated according to an ancient unit of measure. Those stories given a "shekel" rating are only hard, those that merit a "mina" are a bit harder, and those that are given a whopping "talent" are the hardest—or heaviest—of all.

Most of these stories have been written from the perspective of newer Bible translations such as the New International Version. When differences arise in names between newer translations and the King James Version, the alternate spelling is included in parentheses throughout the answer section.

It's been said that God is in the details. After working through *The Bible Detective*, you will appreciate the Scriptures—God's inerrant Word—as you never have before.

ON THE FIRST DAY...

Zuriel rushed to the center of town with his scribe in tow. "Hurry, Gershon, we're going to be late! I can see the people gathering around the rabbi already!"

Gershon grumbled to himself as he struggled to keep up with the frantic Zuriel. He didn't see what the big deal was. Sure, Rabbi Ithamar had an impeccable reputation as a scholar and speaker, but the topic of the big meeting didn't interest him. Zuriel, on the other hand, didn't want to miss a word of the rabbi's lecture on the creation of the world. That is why he brought Gershon, his scribe, to record the rabbi's words on scrolls he had purchased for just this occasion.

Zuriel pushed his way through the people, dragging Gershon by the tunic, to get within earshot of Rabbi Ithamar. "Now, don't you miss a word," Zuriel whispered to Gershon as the rabbi began his lecture. Gershon plopped down on the edge of a nearby well. He took his materials out as Zuriel shot him a warning look implying that the job had better be taken seriously.

"Unclean! Unclean! We have all been made unclean because of the fall of Adam and Eden," the rabbi shouted. "Listen closely as I tell of the state of perfection that the world was created in." Zuriel listened intently, and

9

Gershon wrote hastily, as the rabbi began to teach.

"On the first day God created light and darkness. On the second day He created land and sea, and on the third day He separated the earth and sky. God created the sea creatures and every kind of bird on the fourth day, and then on the fifth day He created the sun, moon, and stars so that the fish and the birds could tell the difference between night and day. And finally, on the sixth day our God and Father created animals and people to rule over all life on the earth."

Zuriel looked puzzled. He scratched his head while he reviewed the rabbi's words. In his own research he had come to conclusions quite different from what the rabbi was teaching. When he noticed Gershon didn't seem to have the same concerns, Zuriel turned his attention back to the rabbi.

"God created the world in six days," Rabbi Ithamar continued, "and on the seventh day He saw that His work was good and caused a great celebration to take place. The world was truly a magnificent place on that day, and it is our responsibility, once again, to achieve that perfection in our own lives."

As the rabbi continued to teach, Zuriel's mind began to drift, and then so did he. With a disgusted look, he motioned to Gershon to follow him. Surprised, Gershon hurriedly packed his materials and left the well where he had been sitting.

"Master, why are we leaving?" Gershon shouted as once again he tried to keep up with Zuriel.

Zuriel responded without looking back. "You were right about not wanting to listen to the rabbi. We're better off doing our own research."

WHY WAS ZURIEL
DISGUSTED WITH
THE RABBI?
(Hint: See Genesis 1–2.)

LOST INNOCENCE

LEVEL OF DIFFICULTY: SHEKEL (HARD)

"Mama, what is innocence?" asked Ben-Joseph.

"Innocence?" repeated his mother. "Why are you worried about inno. . .have you been hiding in the synagogue again?"

One look at her little boy's face was answer enough. "Ben, you know you are too young to sit in on the lessons," she continued. "Why do you keep going back? It will be your turn soon enough."

"I just crawled under the curtain in the back. Grandfather saw me. He was sitting on a bench, and I stuck my head out right under the bench. He didn't make me leave."

Mama sighed. "So what did you learn?" She was glad to have a son who was interested in learning, even if what he really needed to learn was patience.

"Well, they talked about Adam and Eve and that evil snake. You see," he began as if his mother had never heard the story, "the evil serpent spoke to Eve one day and asked about God's rules for the garden. The serpent didn't really know what he was talking about because he said that God wouldn't let them eat from any trees.

"Eve spoke right up and corrected the serpent. She said they could eat from all the trees except the tree that was on the far eastern border of the garden. (I think that's because it was the side closest to Jerusalem.) Eve told the serpent that if they ate from that tree they would get kicked out of the garden for good—"

"I'm thinking that wily snake had something to say about that!" Ben's mother interrupted.

"Very good, Mama! He did! He told her she wouldn't get kicked out at all. So he was calling God a liar right there in God's garden! That snake told her that if she ate of that tree she would become perfect like God and would be able to see into the future.

"And do you know what she did, Mama?" Ben-Joseph asked.

"What?" asked Mama with alarm.

"She ate the fruit from that forbidden tree, and then she gave some to Adam."

"And did Adam eat as well?" Mama hid her eyes as she asked.

Ben shook his head sadly. "I'm afraid he did," he answered. "And then the strangest thing happened. They opened their eyes, I guess for the first time, and saw that they didn't have any clothes on! When they realized that, they put together palm leaves to make some kind of jungle suit. That's when the rabbi spoke about innocence."

Mama leaned forward. "What did the rabbi say?"

"He said they lost the innocence for all of us, and we've never gotten it back."

Mama thought for a minute about Ben's original question. "I guess innocence is the wisdom not to want to know how to do wrong and to be happy just doing right."

"Are you saying I lose my innocence when I sneak into the synagogue?" Ben asked sheepishly.

"No, Ben. From the facts in your story, I think you should sneak into the synagogue a little more often—and don't take any naps under Grandfather's bench!"

HOW DID MAMA
KNOW THAT BEN
MIGHT HAVE SLEPT
THROUGH SOME OF
THE STORY OF
EVE'S TEMPTATION?
(Hint: See Genesis 2–3.)

BROTHERLY LOVE

LEVEL OF DIFFICULTY: SHEKEL (HARD)

As the sun blazed down on the fields of grain, Thomas leaned on his hoe and wiped his brow. *I must hurry and finish this row before the sun goes down,* he thought. *How will I ever support a family if I can't even get this simple chore of tilling the ground done for my father?*

As Thomas stood there lost in his thoughts, his brother Jacob joined him with a flask of water. "Come, Thomas, take a break and join me in a bit of refreshment," Jacob offered.

"No, I can't stop yet. . ." Thomas began.

"Come, come, you look weary. Besides, I have an interesting story to share with you," his brother replied.

"All right," Thomas answered.

Jacob handed his brother the flask and began his story. "I was sitting with Father and some of the local men last night around the campfire, discussing local politics, when the subject of heritage came up. You remember Seth, don't you? Well, his grandson Machir was there and he told us of his grandfather's brothers, Cain and Abel.

"Cain and Abel were the sons of Adam and Eve. Abel, the shepherd, was the oldest; and Cain, the farmer, was the youngest. Apparently both brothers brought offerings before the Lord. Cain brought the first fruits

15

of his crop, the best there was, while Abel only offered a tiny lamb. The Lord was pleased with Cain but disappointed in Abel's offering.

"When the Lord saw that Abel was disturbed by the Lord's response, the Lord asked Abel why he was angry. 'If you do well, will you not be accepted?' God asked Abel.

"Later that day, Abel led Cain out to where he would guard his flocks and murdered him. When the Lord saw what Abel had done, He declared that Abel would be responsible for tilling the land and watching the sheep. He would be a servant to the ground, which would never till properly for him.

"Can you imagine a man ever being so evil as to kill his own brother?" Jacob asked Thomas.

"Yes, I can," Thomas answered, "but you are mistaken in your story."

WHAT MISTAKES
DID THOMAS
NOTICE IN
JACOB'S STORY?
(Hint: See Genesis 4.)

Up in Smoke

There's a wrinkled old man who sits cross-legged in the desert beside a sand dune. Occasionally a traveler will pass by on the nearby road that is overgrown with weeds but only on his way to another place. No one deliberately comes to this place anymore.

One day an archaeologist passed by the old man and his dune. He offered the man a bit of water and asked, "What used to be under that sand dune, Sir?"

"It was a beautiful place," answered the old man.

"What happened?" the archaeologist fired back.

"It was destroyed by God," said the man with tears in his eyes.

The archaeologist knelt beside the man. "And why do you sit here beside a place that was destroyed by the hand of God Himself?"

"Because it is the only home I ever knew," was the simple answer.

"My name is Ishmael," said the passerby as he sat down. "Tell me about the destruction of your home."

The desert dweller seemed grateful for companionship. "It was a lovely, righteous place, a place of worship and freedom. It was my home, and my family was there. We always believed that its destruction had something

17

to do with Lot, the grandson of Abraham, who came to live among us. The night before the fire fell he welcomed foreigners into his home."

"Do you think the foreigners started the fire that destroyed your home?" Ishmael prompted.

"I don't think two men could have started a fire big enough to destroy two cities in one night. I must admit, though, that I was not there when it happened. I had a herd of goats outside the city. When the foreigners arrived, my herd was spooked and scattered. I left town just as a mob of men gathered at Lot's house to inquire about the guests. I spent all night searching for the herd. I saw fire in the sky that night and was grateful for the light it gave me to search by. The next morning this place was an ember, and all my friends and family were gone."

"Why would you blame Lot, if he were destroyed with them?" asked Ishmael.

"I've heard stories since then. I've heard of descendants of Lot. I've got a feeling that he may have escaped the fire. If he did, then the lives of my family are on his head."

Ishmael stood up to leave. "Thanks for the story, old man," he said as he dusted the sand off the back of his clothes. "Your story sounds familiar in many ways to the stories I've heard of the cities of Sodom and Gomorrah. If those are the cities you call home, though, I'm afraid you must have forgotten some rather important details."

WHAT PARTS OF THE MAN'S STORY DID NOT FIT THE ACCOUNT OF THE DESTRUCTION OF SODOM AND GOMORRAH?
(Hint: See Genesis 11, 18–19.)

TRADE RIGHTS

LEVEL OF DIFFICULTY: SHEKEL (HARD)

That came from the land of Edom," explained Jahleel's big brother, stroking an animal skin that hung on the wall.

"Eat 'em?" asked Jahleel. "Where's the land of 'eat 'em,' and what do you get to eat?"

"No, Jahleel. *E-dom*. E-d-o-m. Edom. It's a place to the north of us. Papa brought this skin from there last month. Why do you always have food on your mind?"

"I don't always have food on my mind," Jahleel contested in true kid-brother fashion. "It just sounded like you were talking about eating something. What kind of name is Edom, anyway, if it doesn't have to do with food?"

"Well, in a roundabout way, I guess Edom does have to do with food," said his big brother thoughtfully. "I remember Papa telling us the story of the Edomites. You were probably too young to remember."

Jahleel turned away. "Here we go with the 'too young to remember' stories. I think you make up these stories and then tell me I was too young just so I'll believe you."

"Do not," said Jahleel's brother in disgust.

"Do too," responded Jahleel turning back around. "Anyway, tell me the story."

Jahleel watched his brother lay his head back on his

hands before he answered. "Edom was a nation of people that all came from one man. That man's name was Esau."

"He saw?" clarified Jahleel.

"E-sau. E-s-a-u," explained an exasperated big brother. "Esau was a twin. His brother was Isaac, the famous promised son of Abraham. Isaac and Esau were constantly in competition. Esau loved to be outdoors hunting and building things. Isaac loved to be indoors cooking and making things.

"One day Esau came into the house from an excursion—"

"What's an excursion?" interrupted Jahleel.

"It's like a nature walk; now stop interrupting! Esau came in, and he was so-o-o-o hungry. Isaac had just made a big steak. It must have smelled really good to Esau because he begged Isaac for a piece of it. Isaac was ready with a bargain for Esau. Isaac told Esau that he could have some steak if he sacrificed his birthright.

"A birthright," Jahleel's brother explained, "was a big thing back then. Whoever was the oldest got the biggest inheritance and got to lead the family. Esau had been born just a few minutes before Isaac, so he owned the birthright. Now Isaac was asking to have that birthright for a simple meal."

"Do you have our birthright since you are the oldest?" asked Jahleel.

"Not like in the olden days when this happened. Anyway, as the story goes, Esau did trade his birthright to Isaac that day. It was a foolish choice and one that he lived with the rest of his life. God gave Esau the land that is to the north of us. He went there and started his own clan. God gave him the name Edom, and so Esau's descendants are the Edomites."

Jahleel's brother turned to look at him. "Now do you understand?" he asked. He didn't expect an answer, though. Jahleel had fallen asleep before the end of the history lesson.

DID JAHLEEL'S
BROTHER TELL
AN ACCURATE STORY?
(Hint: See Genesis 25.)

Remembering Joseph

Level of Difficulty: Shekel (Hard)

I am an old woman now, senile, and with just half a memory. But I still remember Joseph. I can see him as a young man, strong and tanned. For a short time he was the desire of my heart.

I was a married woman, mind you, and I'm not proud of my actions. My husband was a rich and powerful man named Potiphar. There was nothing I wanted that I couldn't have—until I met Joseph. I think my husband hired him on the referral of a friend. Not only was he gorgeous, he was a man of integrity, solid inside like stone, and an up-and-comer as well. You know the kind: put him anywhere and he would excel. In my husband's household, Joseph quickly rose to the top as the chief servant—and chief in my affections.

First, I flirted. Then, I cajoled. Finally, I demanded that he be with me. I was foolish, wasn't I? No man of any substance would betray his master by being with his master's wife. What was I thinking?

I wasn't thinking at all.

The time that I finally threw myself completely at Joseph was the last time I ever saw him in my own home. He ran away so fast that he left his shoes right there on the floor. I felt unwanted and betrayed, so I lied to my husband, and he had Joseph put in jail. At first I felt vindicated, but in my heart I knew I had betrayed a man who had done no wrong.

I kept up with Joseph, from a distance, for the rest of his life. I bribed guards for gossip. I bent the ear of many a palace courtier. What I learned never surprised me. Joseph rose to the top, even from a prison cell. His character was so sound that the jailer eventually trusted him with the other prisoners. Once I heard that Joseph had interpreted dreams for two of the king's servants. I believe it was the king's butcher and baker. They had some wild dreams that I would have interpreted as coming from a fever or some potion. But Joseph interpreted the dreams wisely, helping the men to be reinstated in the palace. I felt then that Joseph's break into government had come, and it had.

The butcher and the baker returned to the castle and bragged to the king himself, the high Pharaoh, about what Joseph had done. The king was so impressed that he called Joseph to the palace and gave him a position as cupbearer. Once Joseph was in the palace working for the king, it was no time until he was second-in-command of Egypt.

When I was young I wouldn't have given two mites for a man's integrity. Now that I am old, while I might forget the details of a man's life, what I do remember is the character that shined through.

WHAT DETAILS OF JOSEPH'S CLIMB TO THE TOP HAS POTIPHAR'S WIFE REMEMBERED WRONGLY?

(Hint: See Genesis 37–41.)

ROLLIN' DOWN THE RIVER

The smoke from the fire floated up in circles toward the sky. Three shepherds stared at the bright flames as they ate their simple but hearty dinner. Their conversation eventually led to their good friend Reuel.

"I heard that his daughter married an Egyptian," said Samuel.

"Which daughter?" Seth asked.

"Zipporah," Samuel replied. "She's already borne him a son. Reuel is a good man, and he loves his new son-in-law, Moses, very dearly."

Basham chimed in. "I hear he has an interesting past. Apparently, he is not really an Egyptian, but was raised by the Pharaoh's daughter. He is actually of the house of Edom. When he was born, male babies were being slaughtered, so his mother hid him. They say that after six months she couldn't hide him in the house, so she made a little boat out of a basket and floated him in the Nile."

As Seth's jaw dropped open from astonishment, Samuel picked up the story. "As I understand it, the handmaidens to the Pharaoh's daughter were bathing near the water. They rescued Moses and brought him to their mistress to ask what they should do. The princess adopted the baby and gave him the name Moses. Have you ever heard anything like that?"

"Why is this man here with Zipporah, then?"

Samuel explained. "Moses grew up and saw the cruelty the Egyptians showed to his people. He killed an Egyptian in defense of one of his Edomite countrymen. Moses then fled from Egypt to Kadesh-Barnea, and that's where he met Reuel."

"I have heard," Basham said, "that Moses will be the one who will lead the Edomites out of captivity from Egypt."

"Why would God choose Moses?" asked Seth.

Samuel laughed. "It would seem that is the same question that Moses is asking. They say an angel of the Lord came to him in the form of a dark storm and told him to lead his people out."

Seth looked incredulous. "Are you saying that God came to Moses in the form of a thunderstorm? You cannot be serious. I'd have to talk to Moses myself to believe that."

DID SAMUEL
AND BASHAM
HAVE THEIR
STORIES STRAIGHT?
(Hint: See Exodus 2-3.)

FIGHTING LIKE BROTHERS

LEVEL OF DIFFICULTY: SHEKEL (HARD)

Just outside of Jericho two paths joined into one and then led to the center of town. From one direction came a rabbi, and from the other, a priest. The rabbi was muttering to himself, and so the priest walked along with him once their paths had joined and asked if he could help in some way.

"I'm trying to solve a riddle," said the rabbi. "It's vexing me to the point of despair."

"Tell me then, Brother," the priest requested, "and together we'll find a solution."

The rabbi sighed wearily. "It goes like this: Brothers, two. Sometimes cross. They tricked. They tried. They walked away." The rabbi held his hands out to the side with a shrug.

"Now that shouldn't be so hard, should it?" asked the priest. "Could it be any brothers?"

"I think they are brothers in the Bible. I tried Cain and Abel. They were cross. I guess they tricked, but Abel didn't walk away."

"Maybe you should think about New Testament brothers. What about James and John? They were called the 'sons of thunder,' so they must have been cross at times."

"I thought of them," replied the rabbi, "but they never walked away."

"They walked away from their lives as fishermen," offered the priest weakly. "What about Joseph and Benjamin?"

"They don't work at all," said the rabbi flatly.

"I know! Esau and Jacob!" exclaimed the priest. "They were cross, and Jacob was tricky, and they walked away from each other."

"But then Jacob came back home," corrected the rabbi. "I don't think they fit."

The two men continued on their path toward town. They happened upon a branch that had fallen from a tree. The branch had small buds growing along its bark.

The rabbi picked up the branch. "I know who it is!" he said with a smile.

WHO WERE
THE BROTHERS
AND WHY DID
THE STICK GIVE
AWAY THE
SOLUTION TO
THE RIDDLE?
(Hint: See Exodus 4;
Numbers 17.)

PARTING THE RED SEA

"Grandpa, tell me a story about Moses," little Hamor sleepily whispered to his favorite storyteller.

"I don't know, Hamor. You seem pretty tired."

"No, it's okay, Grandpa. Just a short one, please?"

Hamor's grandfather nodded as he pulled Hamor up onto his lap to settle in for story time. "How about if I tell you about the time that Moses parted the Red Sea?" Hamor cuddled closer in response.

"It happened this way. Moses escaped from the Egyptians with all of the Israelites who had been held captive for so long. Pharaoh, who was the leader of the Israelites, told them that they could leave to return to their homeland, but as they were leaving, the Egyptian people disagreed with Pharaoh. The Egyptians chased after the Israelites to force them to return, even though Pharaoh tried to talk his people out of such a rash response. The Egyptian people had hard hearts and wouldn't listen to Pharaoh, so they gathered together and took with them six hundred of Egypt's best chariots, each being led by a commander. As the army approached, the Israelites noticed them and began to complain that Moses had led them into the wilderness to be killed.

" 'Moses,' one of the men shouted, 'the Egyptians

are following us! Now what are we going to do?'

" 'Don't be afraid,' Moses answered, 'the Lord will rescue us.'

" 'How can He rescue us from this situation? We're about to run right into the Red Sea, and the Egyptians are almost here! I would rather be in slavery in Egypt than stranded in the wilderness with our enemies about to attack!'

" 'Be calm,' Moses replied.

"But the Israelites were not comforted by Moses. Because they believed in their own strength over the strength of God, they decided to make a plan. Sihon, one of the men in the group, whispered to his friend, 'Let's come up with a plan. Maybe if we split up we'll be able to escape.' So Sihon led half the group, and Abar led the other half.

"Moses desperately tried to unite the two groups. He was able to convince Abar and his followers to trust God. Approaching the edge of the water, the thunder rolled and the lightning crashed as Moses raised his staff above the waters. To everyone's amazement, the seas parted so that the Israelites could walk through on dry land.

"Looking behind them as they hurried through the sea, the people watched the Egyptians approaching. The spirit of the Lord empowered them to reach the other side of the sea before the Egyptians could catch them. There was much rejoicing and giving thanks as the last Israelites stepped clear of the sea. Then a loud voice was heard from the sky that said, 'Moses, raise your hand over the sea again, and the waters will rush back over the Egyptian army.' The whole gathering of the Israelites held their breath as Moses raised his hand. Sure enough, the waters crashed over the Egyptians and set the captives free."

WHAT'S WRONG
WITH GRANDPA'S
STORY?
(Hint: See Exodus 14.)

In the Presence of Jehovah

LEVEL OF DIFFICULTY: SHEKEL (HARD)

I t was a mystery," explained Zebulun.

"It was a miracle," corrected his wife, Katarina.

"Are they not at times the same?" he questioned, looking at his guest, who only smiled.

Katarina began to gather the breakfast dishes from the table where she, her husband, and their guest had been sitting. "I'm only saying that when a man goes to the top of a mountain, speaks to God face to face, and comes back down with a glowing face, that's a miracle." She glanced at both of the men as she bustled out of the room.

Zebulun smiled at his guest after Katarina left. "Sometimes, if we don't disagree, we can find nothing to talk about."

"Tell me about this mystery," said the guest.

Zebulun leaned forward. "It is always a mystery when Jehovah shows His face. With Moses on the mountain, it was the greatest mystery of all. God calls a man to a mountaintop. God writes down ten rules for living. For thirty days and nights they commune. Then God Himself prepares a banquet of food to sustain that man. What would you call that, if not a mystery?"

Katarina walked in to gather the water pitcher. As she passed by the table she quietly said, "I'd call it a half myth, the way you tell it."

Zebulun ignored her. "Then that man comes down the mountainside and retains the light of the glory of God on his face. That glory shines so brightly that the man has to wear a veil so he doesn't frighten his countrymen. I call that a mystery."

"I would have to agree with you," the guest said turning his head to spot Katarina as she returned to the table.

"If you would agree with this old man, then you have much to learn," she corrected. "Now I will tell you how it really happened."

IF KATARINA
IS CORRECT,
HOW WILL HER
STORY DIFFER
FROM ZEBULUN'S?
(Hint: See Exodus 34.)

GOD TALKS TO A LITTLE BOY...
BUT HOW?

LEVEL OF DIFFICULTY: SHEKEL (HARD)

Some said that the boy Samuel was sleeping at home beside his mother's bed when he heard the voice. Others said that he was at the tabernacle sleeping at the foot of the high priest Eli's mat. Still others said he was on a journey and was sleeping beneath the stars.

Some said that Samuel recognized God's voice as soon as he heard it. Others said that God revealed His name to Samuel. Still others said that Samuel heard God three times, and then Eli helped him understand that God was speaking.

Some said that Samuel responded to God with holy silence. Others said that Samuel responded to God with the words, "Holy, Holy, Holy." Still others said that Samuel responded with the words, "Speak, Lord. I am listening."

Some said that God's message to Samuel was a message of forgiveness. Other said it was a message of judgment. Still others said it was a prophecy of the Messiah.

Some said that when Eli heard God's message, he danced before the Lord. Others said that when Eli heard the message, he threw Samuel from the temple. Still others said that Eli fainted when he heard God's words through Samuel.

WHAT IS
THE TRUTH
ABOUT SAMUEL?
(Hint: See 1 Samuel 3.)

THE GIANT

LEVEL OF DIFFICULTY: SHEKEL (HARD)

"I hate being the youngest and smallest," Jonathan cried loudly. "I can't do anything," he sobbed.

"Why, Jonathan," his mother replied, "there are a great many people who are small but who accomplished great things. Look at the faithfulness of David, the youngest son of Jeremiah of Bethlehem. I heard today at the market how he showed his great strength in battle.

"Apparently his older brother went off to war and was gone for a very long time," his mother continued. "Jeremiah sent David to the battle area with provisions for his brother, Eliab, and the troops. David, a Philistine, learned that they must send someone to fight Goldar, a huge Israelite man with a head the size of six cubits and a span. Goldar declared that if the Philistines could defeat him, his people would be their servants, but if he defeated the Philistines, then they would serve Israel.

"When David heard about this, he offered his services. David said that he would have no problem defeating Goldar because he had killed men twice his size. David was confident in his capabilities because of his faith in the Lord. King Saul was hesitant. He offered the young warrior a suit of armor, but David refused.

"David approached Goldar with only his staff, a

bow, and shepherd's bag full of arrows. As David approached Goldar, he shouted, 'You come to me with a sword, with a spear, and with a javelin, but I come to you in the name of the Lord of hosts, whom you have defied. This day the Lord will deliver you into my hand!'

"David ran toward Goldar and shot an arrow at his forehead, knocking the giant to the ground. David then ran over to the large man, struck him, and used the giant's sword to cut off his head. Upon seeing David's amazing act of bravery, the Philistines rejoiced!"

"That is an amazing tale, Mother," Jonathan said, "but why do I feel as though you have confused a few of the details?"

WHY DID
JONATHAN QUESTION
HIS MOTHER?
(Hint: See 1 Samuel 17.)

A SUFFERING SAINT

An old man named Bildad was found dead in his rocker just before the Sabbath. On his side table was a parchment note that may have been from a famous man of God. Can you determine its authenticity?

Dear Eliphaz, Bildad, and Zophar,

I am writing to thank you for your visit of comfort and reassurance. You might remember that I had gone through such a time of loss. My three sons and seven daughters had been killed in an enemy attack. A fire destroyed all my sheep and many servants. The Chaldeans stole my camels and killed even more servants. Finally, after all that, I was struck with sores all over my body. Even my wife told me to give up on God's goodness.

I must admit I began to doubt myself throughout this series of tribulations. And so, it was with a grateful heart that I accepted you, my friends, into my home to encourage and to strengthen me. I will long remember our time together as sweet and precious, an island in a storm of fear and doubt.

I live alone now in poverty. Yet I comfort

39

*myself with the memory of your encourage-
ment. Without it, I might have failed God in
the greatest test of my life.*

*Come soon and know that you will be
remembered fondly and welcomed with open
arms.*

Sincerely,
Job

IN YOUR
EXPERT OPINION,
IS THIS AN
AUTHENTIC LETTER
FROM JOB?
(Hint: See Job 1–3.)

In the Lions' Den

LEVEL OF DIFFICULTY: SHEKEL (HARD)

The wise men sat at the city gate, swapping stories, one-upping each other with the wonders they had seen. The older the man, the wilder his stories were. What began as amazing accounts often became tales of bizarre, distended miracles.

Shmuel often passed by the gate to listen and smile. Never once did he correct his elders. Never once did he show disrespect for their foolishness. He loved hearing their imagination at work and, more than that, he loved their fierce dignity. He only wished they could celebrate God's glory for what it was, without embellishment or exaggeration.

"That's nothing," Shmuel heard Eli say. "My great-grandfather was there when they dragged Daniel out of the lions' den."

Audible gasps were heard all around.

"Yes, indeed," Eli continued. "You remember the details, don't you? The evil satraps had convinced the Pharaoh to claim himself god for a year. That's right, for a whole year no one could pray to anyone but the king."

The other men muttered their disgust.

Eli waited for their murmurs to subside. "We all know there was no way that Daniel could have gone a year

41

without praying to Jehovah. Why, the Scriptures themselves teach that Daniel prayed at least ten times a day!

"But we all know the laws of that evil country. Even the king himself could not change one of his own laws. How it must have grieved that king to punish such a good man as Daniel! But punish him he did. His minions threw Daniel into a den of lions. Then they lit a fire at the mouth of the cave to trap Daniel inside and incite the lions into a frenzy.

"In the morning when they cleared away the debris and ash, what do you think they saw? There was Daniel, cradled in the paws of the most ferocious lions!"

"Ah!" said the other men. "And what happened to the king?"

Eli nodded in approval. "The king was so relieved to find Daniel well that he named him his successor!"

"And the evil satraps?"

Eli looked down sadly. "The satraps did not fare so well. They were thrown into the den of lions, along with their wives and children. Unlike Daniel, they were all eaten alive before they even touched the ground of the den."

The others shook their heads sadly. Shmuel shook his head as well but partly in amazement that old wise men would enjoy such an exaggeration of an already wonderful tale.

WHAT WERE
ELI'S
EXAGGERATIONS?
(Hint: See Daniel 6.)

GIFTS OF THE MAGI

LEVEL OF DIFFICULTY: SHEKEL (HARD)

I tell you, there were three wise kings who searched out the child Messiah!" declared Misha. "Don't you remember the three gifts: gold, frankincense, and myrrh? Of course there were three." Misha crossed her arms and nodded her head, daring her cousin, Darius, to contest her.

Darius may have been only eleven years old, but he already recognized when a woman, even if she were his cousin, required gentle treatment. "Misha, please understand, it's not that I doubt your knowledge of the Scriptures. You are exactly correct that there were three gifts. I'm only suggesting, if you don't mind, that maybe the fact that there were three gifts doesn't automatically mean there were three Magi. Maybe, just maybe, the number of gifts has nothing to do with the number of Magi."

In the aftermath of Darius's kindness, the lightning subsided a bit in Misha's eyes. She reconsidered her position. "Darius, how many Magi do you think came to worship and adore Jesus in the manger?"

Darius held his breath. He didn't want to upset his cousin even more. Still, he had to be truthful. "Well, to be honest, Misha, I'm not so sure the Magi were at the manger. I'm thinking they probably came much later to worship."

"Later?" asked Misha. "My dear Darius, you have been here every year as we have celebrated the Christ child with the crèche my papa brought home from Bethlehem. Is it not obvious when you look at it that the shepherds and the wise men all came together to worship the child-king?"

As careful as Darius had been with the temperamental daughter of his Uncle Luca, he now made a fatal error. He laughed. Out loud.

Misha's face clouded over. "Darius? Are you laughing at me?"

"I'm sorry," Darius finally sputtered. "Please don't be angry. I just never heard anyone refer to a woodcarver's nativity scene as the final word on Scripture." He fell into laughter again, holding his belly as he rolled onto the floor.

Misha crossed her arms again and waited. When Darius quieted down enough for her to be heard, she made an attempt to set the record straight. "If you are saying that I do not know the Scriptures, then let me tell you exactly how it all happened. The Magi traveled from the East, following a certain star. When they got to our country, they went directly to King Herod. The king asked many questions and told the Magi to return to him when they had found the child."

"You are correct," said Darius, sincerely wondering how long it would take to make up for his laughter.

Misha continued. "The Magi followed the star until it was directly above the stable where the baby lay. They gave Him their *three* gifts and worshiped the baby.

Before they left town, an angel came to them and warned them that King Herod's intentions were not the best. So they did not go by the palace on their way out of town. They also warned Joseph about impending danger so that he would take the child back to Nazareth for safety."

"Okay," Darius responded hesitantly. "And what did the king do?"

"The evil king ordered all baby boys six months or younger to be killed. He missed the whole point, crazy king."

"Crazy, indeed," responded Darius, and then before he could stop himself, he began to laugh again. "But you, my dear cousin, don't miss the whole point, only some details along the way."

WHAT DETAILS
DID MISHA MISS?
(Hint: See Matthew 2.)

BAPTISM OF A KING

LEVEL OF DIFFICULTY: SHEKEL (HARD)

The fever is still there," Papa said quietly. "It's going to be a long night."

Mama nodded her head in agreement. "It's bad enough that we have to sit up all night with a sick old man. Then he starts ranting and raving, and all of our neighbors have to be up all night with him, too."

Papa smiled. "Let's just hope he doesn't get started on Christ's temptation. Once he gets angry at the devil his voice is unstoppable."

Mama returned the smile. "Let's just hope it's not the tower of Babel. When he tries to shout over all those other languages, I can't even hear myself think."

They both looked down at the old man who had become as dear to them as their own fathers. Mama placed a wet rag across his forehead. It didn't matter how delirious the old man became. They would care for him whenever he needed them. It was a commitment forged through years of laughter and tears.

"It was the River Jordan!" the old man suddenly cried out as Mama and Papa jumped back with a start. "The water was particularly muddy that day."

"It's Naaman and his leprosy," said Mama. "He loves that story."

The old man continued. "The people had gathered at the bank."

"It's the story of our people crossing into the Promised Land," Papa corrected.

"He baptized them one by one," said the old man with his eyes still closed with fever.

"Ahhhh," said the two caregivers in tandem. "John the Baptist."

"You'd better close the shutters," Mama suggested. "This one gets loud."

"John stood by the bank and welcomed believers!" shouted the old man. "He prepared the way of the Lord!"

Knowing they had done all that they could to comfort and care for the old man, Mama and Papa sat down to wait out the fever and the story.

"John had just come out of the River Jordan where he was baptizing when, behold, he saw Jesus coming, walking across the water. When Jesus got to the riverbank where John was standing, He bowed low before John and said, 'Baptize Me, My brother.'

"You can imagine that our brother, John, was thrilled to have such an honor. He baptized Jesus, and just then lightning struck, and the sky grew dark. The Spirit of God came down like fire from heaven proclaiming Jesus as the Messiah. And so you see. . . . "

Suddenly, the old man's face relaxed. The fever was breaking, and he had drifted into sleep. Mama and Papa breathed a sigh of relief. They knew their friend would be brokenhearted to know how confused he often was about Scripture. But they knew it was just the fever, and that the old man's faith was strong and true.

HOW MUCH
OF THE OLD MAN'S
STORY WAS THE
RESULT OF HIS FEVER?
(Hint: See Matthew 3.)

THE OBEDIENT STORM

Three religious leaders and a new convert were discussing the life of Christ. Particularly, they were discussing at what point the disciples became convinced of Jesus' deity.

"I say it was at the Resurrection," said the rabbi.

"I say it was at the feeding of the five thousand," said the Pharisee.

"I say it was when He raised Lazarus from the dead," said the temple priest.

"I think you're all wrong," stated the new convert flatly. "The miracle that convinced the disciples that Jesus was more than just a man was when He calmed the storm. Don't you remember?

"Jesus was sitting on the upper deck keeping watch while his disciples rested below," the new convert continued. "A big storm fell around them. The storm was so rough that the disciples finally awoke and, in fear, ran up to the deck to find Jesus sitting with His face into the wind enjoying the rain and the lightning.

"The disciples called out to Jesus, 'Lord, save us. We're all going to die in this storm!'

"Jesus told them how small their faith was, and then told the wind and the waves to be calm. The storm subsided immediately. That was when the disciples knew that Jesus was no ordinary man. The Scriptures say that they asked each other what kind of man this was. Don't you remember?"

"You haven't got the story exactly right," said the rabbi.

"Yes, you missed a few details," added the Pharisee.

"But you seem to have a grasp of the big picture," said the temple priest.

WHICH DETAILS
DID THE NEW
CONVERT MISS?
(Hint: See Matthew 8.)

Mustard-Seed Faith

The children loved to see Obed the gardener coming down the road. He had deep pockets sewn into his tunic, and there were always surprises inside each one for the children—sometimes sweets to eat, sometimes lessons to learn. With Obed, you could never be sure what was coming next.

On one bright, sunny afternoon Obed came upon some children resting beside a beautiful, yellow field of mustard plants. They called to him, "Obed, come talk to us! What is in your pockets today?"

Obed smiled, and his eyes became brighter. Slowly he made his way across the dirt path to the children.

"Sit down here with us," the children suggested. "Then we can talk the whole day long."

Obed laughed out loud at the innocence of children who didn't understand old bones and low places. "Thank you, but not today. I will tell you a mystery, though."

The children climbed to their knees to be as close to Obed as possible. "Tell us! Tell us!"

Obed reached into his pocket and pulled out a closed fist. "Guess what I have in my hand."

"A bug!" "A sweet cake!" "A secret message!"

"No, none of those is right," Obed answered. "It is a

mystery. It is the very field you sit beside here."

Their eyes growing wide, the children looked around. "How can we be beside a field that is in your hand?" They began to smile, anticipating a joke, but watched carefully as Obed began to open his fist.

Inside of the wrinkled palm was a tiny seed. "It's a mustard seed," the wise man said. "Inside this seed is the beginning of the beautiful yellow plants in this field. And inside this little seed is the mystery of life, little ones.

"Jesus used a little seed like this one to teach us about faith," he continued. "Do you remember?"

"I do," called out a little boy . "He said that if we had faith like a mustard seed, we could make a mulberry tree move to the top of a mountain. Is that right?"

"Not exactly," answered Obed with a smile, "but oh, so very close. Come walk with me down the road, and I'll tell you what Jesus really said about mustard-seed faith."

So down the road Obed went with his four eager disciples and one little seed.

WHAT EXACTLY
DID JESUS SAY
ABOUT FAITH AND
THE MUSTARD SEED?
*(Hint: See Matthew 17;
Luke 17.)*

How You Gonna Keep 'em Down on the Farm?

Level of Difficulty: Shekel (Hard)

As the sun fell behind the towering mountains, Ana and her little brother Stephen made their last turn on the dusty road toward their home. Soon they saw their younger brother and sister playing under a tree.

"Ana, Ana!" the children shouted. "What did Jesus say? What stories did He tell?"

"Hush, and I will tell you," Ana responded. As the children gathered around, she began her tale.

There was once a father who loved his two sons dearly. Eventually, though, the older son grew restless of living at home. One day he asked his father for his part of the family wealth. After obtaining his share, he journeyed to a country nearby where he donated all of his money to those in need. Because he gave all of his money away, he was forced to work in the fields with cattle. His stomach ached every day from hunger. He longed to eat the pods the livestock ate. As the older son stared at the cows feasting on their supper, he grew restless for home. He felt foolish. He knew that he might starve if he didn't return home.

A few days later he did just that. When he arrived, he was greeted by his father and given a robe, a ring for his finger, and fine sandals for his feet. That afternoon, the father began preparations for a feast in honor of his older son's return.

Before long, the younger son who was working in the fields started for home. As he neared the house, he heard music and dancing, and got the story from a servant. He was so angry he refused to join in. A few minutes later his father begged him to come inside.

"How can you honor my brother, while I have dedicated my life to serving you, Father?" the son cried.

The father replied. . . .

"Ana, you know very well that is not how Jesus told that parable," Stephen scolded his sister.

WHY DID
STEPHEN QUESTION
ANA'S STORY?
(Hint: See Luke 15.)

SISTERS

Eva stopped Esther on her way to the well. "Did you hear that Jesus of Nazareth was at Mary and Martha's house last night?"

"Yes, I did," Esther responded. "Martha evidently prepared a feast big enough for half the town."

Eva continued on until she passed Rhoda. Eva asked, "Did you hear about Jesus being at Martha's last night and the meal she prepared?"

"Yes, I did," Rhoda answered. "But did you hear about the big fight Mary and Martha had right in front of everyone?"

Eva filled her ears with information from Rhoda and then filled her water jars with water. Soon Rheza approached her. "Eva, have you heard about the party at Mary's house last night?"

Before Eva even thought about it, she blurted out, "Yes, and Mary and Martha finally had it out. You know how different they are. Martha's always doing, and Mary's always talking. Well, Martha dragged Jesus into the middle of it, and by the time it was over, He had to separate the two."

"I hadn't heard all that," said Rheza. "But I did hear that Martha got so upset that she ruined the supper and offered only fresh vegetables when it came time for the meal."

On her way back to town, Eva passed women talking at every crossroads. She learned something new at each one.

"Mary stormed out of the house with Martha screaming behind her. Lazarus and the men stayed out of it, and they should have," said one woman.

"Jesus told Martha that she was ruining the party," said another.

"Martha said she was moving in with their aunt in Bethel," said still another.

By the time Eva was almost home, she had heard the dinner at Mary and Martha's house depicted as an out-and-out brawl. Eva decided to stop by and see for herself. She walked up to the gate and called out, "Yoo-hoo, Mary? Martha? Anybody home?"

WOULD MARY
AND MARTHA
HAVE DESCRIBED
THEIR INTERACTION
AS THE WOMEN
OF THE TOWN?
(Hint: See Luke 10.)

RESURRECTION IN BETHANY

While the little village of Bethany had a healthy word-of-mouth grapevine for spreading information, there was no formal news information system. The closest thing to a newspaper was the pole in the center of the town square. There you could find notices and news items as well as official decrees. Unfortunately, these items were often erroneous. Take, for instance, this report on a miraculous event in the household of Mary and Martha.

> *Hear ye, everyone! Lazarus was dead, and now he is alive!*
>
> *Just last week our neighbors, Mary and Martha, were mourning the loss of their brother, Lazarus. He had been sick for quite some time. The women had sent for Jesus of Nazareth in the hopes that He could heal their brother before it was too late.*
>
> *Unfortunately, Jesus was unable to come to town until Lazarus had already passed away. In fact, Lazarus had been buried for a week when Jesus finally got to town.*
>
> *According to Martha, she ran to meet Jesus, telling Him that if He had been here, her brother would not have died. Mary wouldn't even speak to her teacher and longtime friend.*

Jesus went to the tomb after speaking with Martha. Once there, He asked that the stone be moved from the entrance. You could understand the townspeople's hesitation since Lazarus's body had been decomposing for a week. Nevertheless, they did as Jesus asked. Jesus then said a prayer heard by everyone. Finally, He spoke the words, "Lazarus, your time has come!"

To the amazement of everyone there, Lazarus walked forth from the tomb fully clothed and in his right mind. There was not a remnant of grave clothes on him. The sisters rejoiced together with their brother and their master at the wonder of this miracle. Many put their faith in Jesus as the long-awaited Messiah.

According to our sources at the temple, there was a meeting shortly afterward involving the Pharisees, the Sanhedrin, and the high priest. Perhaps they are discussing a potential role for Jesus in the priesthood.

WHAT FACTS IN THIS NEWS STORY ARE INACCURATE?
(Hint: See John 11.)

To Be Born Again

Level of Difficulty: Shekel (Hard)

Sarah tried to comfort her friend Mary. "Now there, there's no reason to cry. It was dark, and you were listening through a window. You might not have heard everything in its proper. . .uh. . .context."

"Oh yes, I did," Mary retorted, her eyes turning red from her crying. "He has been acting strangely lately, so I had to follow him. And now, oh, I wish that I hadn't!"

"Well, I think you did hear something wrong," Sarah insisted. "Tell me one more time what you thought you heard, and let's figure this out."

"Okay," agreed Mary reluctantly. "As I said, Nicodemus has been acting like he has something on his mind. He has always confided in me when things trouble him. He is a Pharisee, after all, a responsible man, and he needs the support of his wife.

"So tonight I followed him when he left after supper. He went to see that Jesus character who has been causing such trouble. You know the one who associates with common prostitutes and seedy characters. Then I knew that Nicodemus must be seeing one of those terrible women.

"I admit that they were inside the house and that I couldn't hear everything through the window, but I did hear them discuss, oh, I can't bear to say it. . .a baby."

"A baby!" Sarah exclaimed.

"Yes. I heard Jesus say something about being born, and then Nick replied something about a womb. Jesus seemed to get kind of angry then, and I heard Him chastise Nick by saying, 'Flesh gives birth to flesh.' That just broke my heart.

"Then it got quiet again, so I inched a little closer to the window. That's when I heard Jesus say something about loving and about an only son. After that, I had to run home."

Sarah was shocked and in pain for her friend. "Well, Mary, I suggest that you have it out with Nicodemus tonight when he drags in. You need to find out, face to face, what this is all about and what this man Jesus has to do with it."

Just then Nicodemus came into the room appearing pensive. Seeing his wife's tears he asked, "What's wrong, Mary?"

Without even thinking, Mary replied, "Have you been out with your other woman, or just hanging around with that troublemaker, Jesus?"

Nicodemus replied, "I did go to see Jesus. I asked Him about the miracles He performs and where His power comes from. Then He explained that we must all be born again. He chastised me for not understanding these things already, and He made me a little angry. . . . "

Mary ran crying into the bedroom.

Sarah looked at Nicodemus with disgust. "Can you do no better than that, Nicodemus? Who would believe a story about being born again?"

HOW IS
MARY MISREADING
THE SITUATION?
(Hint: See John 3.)

WHEN THE ROOSTER CROWED

LEVEL OF DIFFICULTY: SHEKEL (HARD)

Delia rushed into the courtyard looking for Marcus. "Did you see that man crying outside?" she asked him.

"What man?" Marcus replied distractedly, looking away.

"The only man who is crying his heart out beyond the gate. Do you know why he's so upset?"

Marcus finally fixed his gaze on his friend. "I don't know what man you are talking about, so I can't know why he is so upset. Do you know what's happening here tonight? It's the trial of that man Jesus who many believe is the Messiah. It's been going on all night. I have never felt such tension here."

"I know why that man is crying," hissed a sly voice. "His name is Peter, and he is undoubtedly a close friend of the man who is on trial." The voice belonged to a woman who went by the name Diana. . .sometimes.

"What do you know about him?" asked Delia, taking a half-step away from the woman.

"I know a thing or two," answered Diana, slowly, hoping for more inquiries.

"How do you know?" prompted Delia.

Diana spat on the ground nearby. "Actually, I followed

63

him. I've become quite good at reading people's intentions. I think he wanted to be inside at the trial, but he was afraid. He sat out in the courtyard instead. A nosy little servant girl asked him if he were a friend of Jesus of Nazareth. This guy, Peter, denied it, but I could tell he was lying. I would wager that even the girl could tell. When he headed into the judgment hall, I followed along just to see what would happen.

"Sure enough, it happened again. The people are so crazy for information, you know. A man told the crowd standing around Peter that he had been a companion of Jesus. This time Peter swore with an oath and claimed not even to know the man. The crowd was stunned at the vehemence of his response. He left the hall and stood at the gate beyond the courtyard. Some in the crowd followed him.

"It didn't take more than a few minutes before somebody called his bluff. They claimed they had seen him with the other disciples. They said he even talked like them. But again, swearing even more severely, he denied knowing this Jesus that everyone was talking about."

Diana shifted her weight as if she were getting bored with her own story. "I can't say that I blame the man. From the sound of it, this Jesus is going to be executed later today. His friends could be in danger."

Delia had listened patiently to all the information, none of which answered her question. "But why, then, was he weeping just outside the gate?"

Diana dropped her voice to a whisper. "All I know is that just after he denied knowing Jesus the fourth time, the sun broke over the horizon. This Peter looked at the sunrise. It seemed to be some kind of sign to him.

I was standing close enough to hear him say, 'Just as He said. . . .' Then he broke into sobs and ran outside.

"I wanted to ask, 'Who said?' But I knew who he was talking about, Jesus of Nazareth, the supposed Messiah. Peter was one of this man's disciples, but he denied it all. His King of glory was being sentenced to death, and he was a coward. Wouldn't you have shed some tears if you were Peter?"

"I don't know what I'd do," Delia said as Diana sauntered away.

"Careful, Delia," said Marcus. "I'm not sure you can trust the stories Diana tells."

WAS DIANA'S
STORY TRUE TO
THE SCRIPTURAL
ACCOUNT?
(Hint: See Matthew 26.)

THE PRICE OF THE CHRIST

LEVEL OF DIFFICULTY: SHEKEL (HARD)

All conversation stopped as the monotone voice of the court officer droned, "All rise. Court is now in session. The people versus Nathan Agabus of the Jerusalem synagogue. The honorable Judge Onias, presiding."

Once everyone was seated, the judge asked the attorney for Nathan Agabus to summarize the case.

"Your Honor," the attorney began, "my client has been unjustly accused of a heinous crime. The charges should be dropped immediately and the case dismissed."

The judge raised his eyebrows. "Counsel has been asked to summarize the case rather than state what my response should be. Please continue and stay on track this time."

"Thank you, Judge," the barrister responded, looking down at his minimal notes. "The night in question is the night that Judas Iscariot approached my client and his colleagues in a greedy attempt to betray his teacher and escape with some money. Now, your Honor, Iscariot is a known penny pincher and lover of money. He is the one who should be tried today, not Mr. Agabus."

"Stick to your summary, please," interrupted the judge with no emotion.

"Of course," said the attorney clearing his throat. "Iscariot alleged that Mr. Agabus approached *him* asking what he would charge to betray Jesus of Nazareth. He also alleged that my client stated that the price for the task would be thirty pieces of silver. Your Honor, please, thirty pieces of silver for a man's life?"

Before the judge could interrupt again, the lawyer continued. "Iscariot alleges that he tried to talk my client and his colleagues out of the transaction before the whole Gethsemane fiasco. Again, so he says, after the execution of Jesus of Nazareth, he returned to the temple to give back the silver he had supposedly been given by Mr. Agabus. Iscariot says that at that point in time he confirmed Jesus' innocence. He says my client responded to that confirmation with a statement in the nature of 'That's your problem.' "

The attorney looked at the judge with a pleading look to express his disdain for the whole proceedings. "Iscariot further alleges that my client did receive back the money, but instead of placing it into the treasury, he purchased a small piece of land, land that is already known as the Field of Blood. Your Honor, is this not all laughable?"

The judge tilted his head slightly to the right. "Barrister, how does your client respond?"

"First of all," the attorney quickly answered, "my client is a fine, upstanding member of the religious leadership. He would not put a price on a man's head. Secondly, he has never been approached by Mr. Iscariot. Lastly, he knows nothing of a purchase of land with any blood money and is willing to lead an internal investigation into the matter if necessary."

"Is Judas Iscariot available for testimony?" the judge asked quietly.

"No, Judge. Mr. Iscariot was found dead yesterday after having hanged himself."

"Hmmm," murmured the judge.

WAS JUDAS
ISCARIOT'S STORY
ACCURATE AS TOLD
BY THE ATTORNEY?
(Hint: See Matthew 26–27.)

ONE PRISONER GOES FREE

The year was A.D. 36. The town was Jerusalem. On a local centurion's wall hung a wanted poster for a notorious criminal with a phenomenal past.

Description:
Medium build, dark hair and eyes,
several scars on his right cheek.

Wanted for:
Murder—Kidnapping—Insurrection
Political terrorism—Disturbing the peace

To all good citizens:
Be on the lookout for this man.
His name is Barabbas,
though he may go by many aliases.

Barabbas was on death row several years ago but was set free on a technicality. He was being held for kidnapping and thievery. Another man, Jesus of Nazareth, was being held for blasphemy and disturbing the peace. That man's arrest was a political coup for the Jewish religious leaders. They felt threatened by the presence of a self-acclaimed Messiah such as Jesus of Nazareth. The crowd at the trial was enraged and bloodthirsty. Caesar, the Roman governor, knew that it was customary to release a prisoner at the Passover festival. In a last-minute attempt to appease the mob, Caesar offered them the choice between Jesus, who had no prior record, and Barabbas, a convicted murderer. Even Barabbas spoke in the man's defense, admitting his own crimes. Still, the crowd chose Barabbas, who was freed that same night before the crucifixion of the innocent Jesus.

Since that time, Barabbas has returned to his life of rebellion and terrorism. He has been associated with the bombings at the temple and the vandalism at the palace.

If you see this man, stay away, but notify the authorities immediately. He is certainly armed and, more certainly, dangerous. WANTED: DEAD OR ALIVE.

FROM WHAT
YOU REMEMBER OF
JESUS' TRIAL,
IS THE ACCOUNT
INCLUDED HERE
ACCURATE?
(Hint: See Matthew 27; Mark 15.)

FRIEND AND FOLLOWER

LEVEL OF DIFFICULTY: SHEKEL (HARD)

Even after Jesus' Resurrection, the Pharisees were constantly trying to find fault with Jesus. They spied on His followers in hope of finding reasons to run them out of town. Occasionally they questioned His friends, trying to appear casual, of course, to dig out information.

"Tell us about this Mary Magdalene," chief Pharisee Lamech asked Joanna.

"What do you want to know?" Joanna shot back. She understood the game Lamech was playing with her, and she didn't appreciate his approach.

"I have heard that she has given actual money to support Jesus' ministry," offered Lamech.

"I have done the same, so if she is guilty of something, so am I," Joanna said confidently. "We care for Jesus and help Him in any way we can. Do you have a problem with that, Lamech?"

"Well, I *am* wondering how much of your money goes into the evangelist's coffers rather than the temple coffers."

Joanna answered not a word.

Lamech retraced his steps and began again. "We have heard that when Jesus first met Mary in Magdala, He cast fifteen demons out of her. Perhaps that is why she is unusually attached to Him."

"How would you feel about someone who had set you free from a life of spiritual bondage, Lamech? Perhaps if you explore that for yourself, you will understand Mary's attachment to her teacher."

Lamech scowled at the insinuation that he would understand spiritual bondage. "I heard she ran away from the crucifixion screaming. Why would a woman respond to a man's death even more dramatically than His own mother?"

Joanna leaned forward and looked her enemy in the eyes. "Lamech, how would I know why one woman responds one way and another responds completely differently? You are the rabbi. You explain it."

"But at least you will not deny," Lamech contested, "that she was one of the first ones to claim that Jesus was risen. The rumor is that she saw Him in the garden and mistook Him for a guard. She is spreading this ridiculous myth far and wide. At least will you admit to that?"

Joanna smiled. "This is what I will admit to. Mary does believe with all of her heart that she met Jesus after His Resurrection in the garden around His tomb. She has spread the joy of that encounter to everyone who would listen. She will probably continue to spread that joy for the rest of her life. If you ask me, Lamech, rather than fighting her, you should get some of that joy for yourself."

DID LAMECH HAVE HIS FACTS STRAIGHT ABOUT MARY?

(Hint: See Matthew 27; Luke 8; John 20.)

A Husband's Lie
and a King's Mistake

LEVEL OF DIFFICULTY: MINA (HARDER)

"I just don't know what I'm going to do!" Abishai, the court scribe, rubbed his hands together in worry. "I couldn't hear him talking that fast, and he was angry, and I was afraid to ask him to repeat himself, and there were so many people running in and out of the room, and. . . ."

"Stop!" said Tmira. "Slow down and tell me what happened at the palace today. What could have been so terrible that you have rubbed the skin from one hand onto the other? Take a breath and tell me step by step."

"That's exactly what I need to do, Tmira. Whew! You are the one person who can help me. You know it's my job to keep the king's log. Usually he dictates this to me in a reasonable way, but today he was like a madman! Since you are a handmaiden in the queen's court, I was hoping that you would know what was going on and could help me decipher these notes of mine."

"I understand," said Tmira with a deliberate calmness. "I tell you what, you read your notes to me, and I'll help you understand them. The court has been crazy enough these last days without even more mistakes in the record."

And so Abishai began:

> *On this day, I, the king, set this record that I am innocent of a wrong that has been committed by a foreigner in my kingdom, Abraham of Ur.*
>
> *Abraham entered my kingdom with a beautiful woman by his side. When asked, he said that this woman was his cousin. As king, I wanted such a beautiful woman to be my own wife, so I sent for her, and she came.*
>
> *Try as I might, though, I couldn't touch this woman. I couldn't make her mine. Last night I understood. God told me in a dream that she is a married woman! A married woman! No wonder God is angry. No wonder He says I'm a dead man!*
>
> *I told God that I had been lied to, that I had not touched her, and that I had been innocent in this situation. That is when God told me what to do. He said to go wash in the Jordan River seven times and then to run Abraham out of the land. After that I would be forgiven.*
>
> *Early this morning I met with my advisers, and we confronted Abraham. His only explanation was that he was afraid we would kill him. He went into a long genealogical explanation about his actual, distant relationship to this woman who was his cousin but is now his wife. But I just sent him on his way with nothing but a farewell.*

When Abishai finished reading, he looked at Tmira with pleading eyes. "Is any of this true? Could a man really have lied about his own wife?"

"That might be one of the few facts you have correct in your notes, Abishai. Let's go back through the record and sort it out."

WHAT ERRORS
DID YOU CATCH
IN ABISHAI'S NOTES?
(Hint: See Genesis 20.)

No Looking Back

Aaron was tired of tourists. He wanted to be left alone in the wilderness to pray and meditate. He wanted to clear his mind of sinful thoughts and try to find Jehovah's will for his life. Aaron had chosen the life of a hermit because he couldn't stand to be around people at all. But there were still these tourists wandering around asking questions.

They all asked the same questions: "Do you know where Sodom and Gomorrah were? Did you see the cities destroyed? What really happened to Lot and his family?"

Aaron was so sick of answering those questions that one day he decided to test the knowledge of a particularly pesky group of tourists.

"I am so glad you asked about Sodom and Gomorrah," he began. "I remember that day well. I was sitting up here on this very hill when a family came out of nowhere and walked right up to me.

"It was a man, his wife, a little boy, and an older girl," Aaron continued. "They had been traveling hard, running by the looks of it, from the north in the direction of the cities. So, of course, I asked them what was happening.

"Well, the man—whose name was Lot, by the way—

said that they were running because God Himself had warned them that He was going to destroy Sodom and Gomorrah due to the wickedness there. The way Lot told it, God had told them to run out on the plain where the destruction wouldn't reach them and not to turn around even to watch. So that's what they did, without hesitation.

"Then, as Lot and I talked, something happened that I would never forget. There was a big explosion in the direction of the cities. It frightened the boy and the poor little thing cried out. Lot's wife turned to help her son, and *poof!* She was salt.

"In fact, that salt pillar right over there is her," Aaron concluded sadly. "Why don't you go over and check it out?"

WAS THE OLD,
GROUCHY HERMIT
HONEST WITH
THE TOURISTS,
OR HAD HE CHANGED
THE STORY OF
SODOM AND
GOMORRAH?
(Hint: See Genesis 19.)

The Wife Hunt

Late at night, after the masters had all gone to bed, the servants of well-to-do households often gathered by a fire, mending sandals and discussing recent events. It was around such a fire that Abraham's servants discussed the newcomer to the house.

"Her name is Rebekah," said one.

"How did he meet her?" asked another.

"We'll know more when Amos arrives," they all agreed.

The group's chatter fell to a hush as Amos joined the circle with his tools. He began sharpening his knife against a well-worn stone.

"Well?" asked Deborah. "Are you going to tell us or aren't you?"

Amos sighed before he looked up. "You're wondering about the young master's new wife, aren't you?"

They all nodded, but no one spoke.

Amos slowly put down his knife. Then he let a slip of a smile pass across his lips. "The house is all in an uproar, isn't it?"

His friends returned his smile but still did not speak. They were hoping for some small bit of information about this new woman in the household.

Amos obliged. "It's quite an amazing story, really. Things have been so much aflutter that I might not have *all* the details straight, but I'll try. You know that Elihu was sent by Master Abraham to find a wife for young Master Isaac. He was to travel anywhere except Abraham's hometown to find a suitable woman.

"After journeying for some time, Elihu arrived at a well with the horses he had taken from our stable. He rested them there, and then he had a novel idea. He decided to ask a woman for water and he prayed for a sign from God. He prayed that the one who carried the water jug on her shoulder to him would be the one for Isaac.

"Elihu asked woman after woman for water, but each time she carried the water to him at her side. Each time he declined the water. Then came Rachel."

"Oh. . .Rachel. . .pretty name," the group murmured among themselves.

"When she came to him with the water jug on her shoulder, Elihu knew that she was the one. He invited himself to her house and met her brother and family. After *much* negotiation he brought her back with him, and the wedding plans are being made!"

AMOS REALLY
DID MISS SOME DETAILS
IN THE UPROAR.
WHILE THE CAMPFIRE
CROWD WOULD REPEAT
AMOS'S STORY TO
EVERYONE THEY
COULD FIND, WHAT
ERRORS WOULD THEY
BE SPREADING?
(Hint: See Genesis 24.)

I'm Dad's Favorite

Father, let me drive the sheep into the field for I'm older and strong in my ways," Matthias stated.

"No, let me, Father, for I am younger and stronger," protested Matthias's younger brother Jody.

"Now, my sons, I shall let each of you take turns," said their father wisely. "I do not want you to compete. I want you to love each other with brotherly love. Let me tell you about two brothers, Jacob and Esau." And then he began his story.

Jacob and Esau were twins born to Isaac and Rebekah. During her pregnancy, the Lord told Rebekah that two nations were in her womb. He said that one people would be stronger than the other and that the younger would serve the older.

Now when Isaac was very old he had trouble seeing. He requested that Jacob go hunting and bring back some delicious food. Rebekah stood outside listening to the request. Because Esau was her favorite son, she devised a plan to help him obtain his father's blessing instead of Jacob. She told Esau to fetch fine linen so she could sew Isaac a beautiful blanket.

While his mother was preparing the blanket,

Esau said to his mother, "My brother is a hairy man, while my skin is smooth. What if Father discovers my deceit and curses me instead of blesses me?"

Rebekah considered this. "Then let your curse be on me," was her only reply. After she finished the blanket, she dressed Esau in Jacob's clothing and placed feathers on his hands and neck to get rid of the smoothness.

Later that night Esau brought the blanket to his father while pretending to be Jacob. Isaac felt Esau's arms and replied, "You sound like Esau. Are you really my son Jacob?"

"Yes, my father," Esau lied.

"Bring the blanket to me, and I shall cover myself in it and sleep peacefully," Isaac instructed Esau. Esau handed him the blanket, and Isaac blessed his son.

Shortly thereafter Jacob returned home from the hunt and brought the prepared food into his father. "Who is it?" Isaac called out.

Dumbfounded, Jacob said, "I am your firstborn."

"What?! Where is the one who brought me the blanket? I rested peacefully underneath it and have blessed him," Isaac cried.

When Jacob heard his father's cry, he began trembling and begged, "Bless me also, Father!"

"I cannot, my son," Isaac said sadly, "for your brother Esau came in deceit and stole your blessing."

After Matthias's father finished his account, he turned to his two sons and said, "See, my sons, it is not good to compete with one another. Look how terribly

Esau treated Jacob."

"While the brothers may have competed, I believe you are mistaken on some of the details, Father," Matthias said.

WHY WOULD
MATTHIAS SAY THAT?
(Hint: See Genesis 25, 27.)

DREAM A LITTLE DREAM...

*W*hat a day, Rabbi Elan thought as he set his satchel down. That morning he had received an interesting letter regarding a young man in Egypt who had the ability to discern dreams. *I wonder if he could help me interpret the dream I had last week.*

Dear Elan,

I am writing you regarding Joseph, son of Edom, a man that Pharaoh holds in high esteem. In fact, Pharaoh has declared that his people should be ruled according to Joseph's word.

Though Joseph is living well now, he has had his share of misfortunes. When Joseph was younger, his brothers were jealous of him. First, they were jealous because Joseph was their father's favorite son. They also were jealous because of the dreams Joseph had. In one of these dreams, he and his brothers were out in the field with their flocks, and all of his brothers' flocks circled his and then bowed down before them. In another, Joseph saw himself as an eagle soaring above his brothers and then perching on a mountaintop.

The brothers plotted to sell Joseph to tribunes

from Rome. *After seeing that the Romans would
have nothing to do with an Edomite, they sold
Joseph to Ramses, an assistant to Pharaoh. In
Ramses's home, Joseph was accused of stealing and
was thrown into prison.*

*While in prison, Joseph used his uncanny ability
to discern dreams. Another prisoner, a former chief
butler in the palace, dreamed of a vine with three
branches that were budding. He saw Pharaoh's cup
in his own hand. He then crushed the grapes into
the cup and placed it in Pharaoh's hand.*

*Joseph believed that the three vines represented
the three governing bodies of Egypt. He said that
crushing the grapes into Pharaoh's cup meant the
butler would be promoted to the position of
Pharaoh's spokesman. What do you think of all of
that, Elan?*

"It is amazing, indeed, Hernon," Elan thought aloud.
"But I heard something different regarding Joseph in the
market the other day. This letter may be inaccurate."

WAS THE
LETTER INACCURATE?
(Hint: See Genesis 37, 39–41.)

Two Brave Midwives

Shiphrah and Puah were on every Hebrew's blacklist. The Hebrew people in Egypt had grown to be a whole nation. This nation began when Jacob moved to Egypt with his twelve sons. From that family grew the Hebrews, a clan so large that the king of Egypt, or the Pharaoh, was afraid the foreigners would one day take over his kingdom. Because of this, he gave an evil order to two midwives. Those two midwives were named Shiphrah and Puah. The order was to kill all Hebrew male babies but to let the females live.

News of the king's order passed through the Hebrew ranks like a fast-burning brushfire. Where once Shiphrah and Puah were welcomed and revered, they were now feared and despised. When they walked down the street, mothers pulled their children closer. When they congratulated an expectant mother, she often avoided many of their questions. It was a difficult time.

When Shiphrah or Puah did help with a delivery, no one spoke of it afterward. Instead of a joyful celebration, each house went into a time of mourning and silence until the whole community felt black with depression.

The king called in Shiphrah and Puah to congratulate them. "Hello, ladies, and thank you for your hard work.

I know my command must have been difficult at times to fulfill, but we will be a stronger nation because of it."

Shiphrah and Puah were silent but respectful.

He continued. "I have seen the contempt that your countrymen have for you. I believe in time that will wane. Will you be able to hold true in the midst of such difficulty?"

Shiphrah spoke for both of them. "If you are pleased thus far, we think we can stay the course. How long, O king, will this continue?"

"Perhaps for a year," was his answer.

The midwives exchanged glances and then bowed deeply. On their way out of the palace they were spit upon by some of their older countrymen. They walked home past houses where children used to play while their mothers watched, but no children played in plain sight anymore.

DID THE
MIDWIVES OBEY
THE KING'S COMMAND?
(Hint: See Exodus 1–2.)

GOD IN A BUSH?

LEVEL OF DIFFICULTY: MINA (HARDER)

The scribe looked up sharply when he heard the door. Who would be there at this time of night? A small and wrinkled old gypsy woman walked around the stacks of books to the front of his desk. In her hand was a parchment that looked almost as ancient as she.

Since she didn't speak, the scribe asked, "Is there something I can do for you?"

She held the parchment out for him to see. "Is it real?"

He took it from her hands. "I guess that depends on what you think it is."

"I think it is Moses's journal from the day he saw the holy bush," she said quietly.

The scribe stopped midmotion and looked into the woman's eyes to see if she were joking. She wasn't. After a moment of hesitation he slowly smoothed out the parchment. "Let's have a read, shall we?"

At first I thought it was a reflection, maybe the sun on a leaf, but then I realized it was a fire. I walked toward the flames, cautious at first, then more curious as I got closer. A bush was on fire. It was burning slowly to the ground but so slowly

90

that it was almost imperceptible.

I moved closer until I heard a voice behind me calling my name, but I couldn't take my eyes off of the bush. The voice called my name and then told me to take off my coat and tunic and come closer. At that moment the voice identified itself as Jehovah God, and I stood and began to run away. But He called me back.

He gave me good news for my people. The days of slavery were about to be over. But He had startling news for me. God wanted to use me to free my people. Me! I was exhilarated that God Himself would choose me. . . .

The scribe stopped reading and looked at the woman sadly. "I don't know who wrote this, Ma'am, but it is not Moses's account. If you knew the Scriptures, you would have known this yourself."

HOW DID THE
SCRIBE KNOW SO
QUICKLY THAT THE
DOCUMENT WAS
A FRAUD?
(Hint: See Exodus 3.)

THE PLAGUES

Zechariah and Reuben, two ornery old men, sat in front of the hearth while their wives prepared a meal in the kitchen. Sarah and Melda chuckled while their husbands continued to debate Israel's history. The two friends had been at it for years, arguing over anything they could still remember.

"I'm telling you," Zechariah angrily declared, "there were ten plagues, not eight!"

"You're wrong, Zechariah," Reuben responded, "and let me tell you something else. When Moses struck the waters with his rod, they turned into wine not blood. You're getting your stories mixed up."

"No, I'm not! You're the one getting your stories mixed up. You probably don't even know when that plague occurred."

"Sure I do," Reuben confidently replied. "It was the second one, right after the boils broke out on all the people and beasts. Then came the lice, frogs, flies, and snakes."

"You're right about the snakes being the sixth plague," Zechariah consented, "but the water being turned into blood was the first plague and then came the frogs, lice, and flies. The boils didn't come until later."

"Well," Reuben grudgingly replied, "at least we

agree about the snakes."

As Zechariah and Reuben began to disagree on another subject, Sarah and Melda discussed their husbands' knowledge of the plagues. "They're at it again, Sarah. How can any two old men be friends for so long and yet argue over half the time that they are together?"

"It's a wonder to me, too," Melda consented. "It seems that each time they differ, one of them has almost all the facts straight, and the other one can't seem to accept it." She lovingly looked at the two men still sitting in front of the hearth and laughed. "At least they always seem to agree by suppertime, whether they are right or not."

WHICH FACTS
DID THE OLD
MEN REMEMBER
ACCURATELY?
(Hint: See Exodus 7–12.)

THE GREAT ESCAPE, AND OTHER MIRACLES

The campfire lit the boys' faces, while just behind them the night seemed a black void. These were the outcasts, the wanderers, those who hadn't found their place. They were all fifteen years old, so they were just babies when their families relocated to. . .nowhere. All of their short lives these boys had been moving tents and carrying suitcases, pulling stubborn mules and leaving behind graves of grandfathers and old aunts. Even in their youth they were weary of carrying a legacy that sometimes felt more like a heavy chain than a promise.

That is why they wandered out from the camp to sit together in the darkness. That is why they talked into the night about what things they wished were different, and how they hoped things would be one day.

"I think I have forgotten why it was so important to leave Egypt," said Dan. "Maybe our parents were slaves, but at least they had something to eat besides these manna cakes every day."

"They say that in Egypt it was very hard work, that many people died," offered Samuel, the quiet one.

94

Dan threw his hands into the air. "People die here! It's difficult *here*, Samuel."

Jacob picked up a dried leaf and tossed it onto the fire. "You know what Moses says. He says to remember our journey. That's why he walks us back through the whole thing in our assemblies. You don't think he'd lie to us, do you?"

"Of course not," answered Dan. "But I hear my mother crying sometimes, and I hate this life."

The boys sat in silence watching the blaze grow weaker. Elias spoke for the first time since they had gathered. "But what must it have been like when they saw those frogs coming over the hills? Can you imagine?" The plague of the frogs, which had occurred in Egypt, was repeated most often during these campfire sessions.

"Think about it," Elias continued as the other boys began to grin, "hundreds of frogs leaping across the ground. There were frogs in the soup, frogs in the wells, frogs in the sacred places."

"Frogs on the horses," added Samuel.

"Frogs in Pharaoh's court," laughed Jacob.

"Frogs in little Egyptian girls' beds," Dan said slyly.

A short distance from the boys, hidden in the dark, an old man smiled to hear their conjecturing.

"Who can remember all ten plagues?" Jacob asked.

"Who could forget," answered Samuel. "There was water to blood, frogs, lice, animal disease, boils and sores, hail, locusts, flies, darkness, and death."

"The plagues were important," commented Dan, "but what I think was awesome was Aaron's rod."

Samuel once again provided the details. "He threw

down the rod. It turned into a snake. The magicians threw down their rods. They all turned into snakes and ate each other up." He took a breath. "What do you think happened after they'd eaten each other and they turned back into rods?"

The boys thought about that before Jacob spoke again. "Then there was the divided sea."

"Indeed," the other two boys said together.

"What must it have been like to walk beside that wall of water on dry ground?" wondered Dan.

"And what must it have been like to hear the water roaring back!" responded Jacob.

"I guess for that time, Pharaoh's armies must have been glad to be stuck on the other side of the sea rather than right behind the Hebrews. They had a story to tell that night, didn't they?"

The boys heard a sound behind them and immediately fell quiet as a fourth face appeared beside the fire. To their amazement, it was Moses himself. The boys began to study their feet as soon as they recognized the leader of their people.

"So this is what you do out here at night," he said, not unkindly. "Forgive me for listening in the dark. I'm glad you understand that remembering our path is the best way to endure our suffering. Could I help you with a few details you may not be remembering exactly right?"

WHAT DETAILS
DO YOU THINK
MOSES WOULD
HAVE CORRECTED?
(Hint: See Exodus 5, 7–8, 14.)

Is this
the Ark of
the Covenant?

Zerubahi was old, but he was more tired than his years. He had been a priest for too long, he reasoned. He had seen the temple torn apart and rebuilt, only to be destroyed again. He had seen his people drift away and return to the Lord, only to drift away again. He was worn out from the stress of a people who didn't seem able to love God in return.

Most mornings he wandered between the temple ruins and the town market. Most afternoons he sat in the shade behind the temple and slept as much of the day away as he could manage.

"Zerubahi, wake up! We have found something important!"

Zerubahi squinted at the small form of a boy in front of him. He couldn't remember exactly where he was or why he was there, so he sat up and looked around. And who could blame him? He was in the middle of his afternoon nap!

"Zerubahi, are you listening? We have found something *important!*"

The priest recognized the face of Jonas, a young boy he had chased out of the temple on several occasions. "Have you been digging through holy rubble again?" he asked with retribution in his voice.

With not the smallest sign of remorse the boy responded, "Yes, and this time you will be so glad."

Zerubahi relaxed against the wall behind him. He tried to recover from such a sudden awakening. "What is it you think you have found?"

At first the boy answered so quietly that his answer was unintelligible. When the priest didn't respond the boy repeated himself, but still quietly. "The Ark of the Testimony from the Holy Place."

Jonas spoke with such awe in his countenance that it was not difficult for the priest to hold back his laughter. The ark had not been around for many years. There was no way that the child and his friends had found it. "Tell me about it."

"We've been digging back in the back of the rubble. Today we found the corner of a metal box. I think it is bronze. There is one big ring on the end of it, I guess for the priests to hold onto when they carry it. It's about three feet long and, I think, about a foot wide. Do you think the Ten Commandments and Elijah's mantle are still in it? Would you come with us to look?"

Zerubahi looked at the boy kindly. "Young man, it would be a wonderful thing if you had found the ark. For our ancestors it was God's presence among them. But from what you have already told me I know that whatever you have found, it isn't the Ark of the Covenant."

Jonas wilted before the priest's eyes. "How do you know?"

HOW DID ZERUBAHI KNOW?
(Hint: See Exodus 25.)

SHOUTING DOWN THE WALLS

LEVEL OF DIFFICULTY: MINA (HARDER)

I sabella! Must you be so loud?" Old Uncle Zechariah shouted from the corner.

The room fell silent, including Isabella.

"But Uncle, I'm only shouting because I'm happy," the girl known as Izzie countered.

"I don't care if you're shouting to fell the walls of Jericho, girl," he began, and then softened his voice. "I just need some quiet." Then he even smiled. "And I think you are just the person to give it to me."

Isabella climbed up onto her uncle's lap, relieved that he was no longer growling like a bear. "I know how the walls fell down around Jericho, Uncle. I've heard the story many times."

Before her uncle could stop her, she began the tale. "You see, Jeremiah was leading the Hebrews into the Promised Land. The first town God told them to capture was the city of Jericho. They carried the altar from the temple and marched around the city. Do you know that they marched around once a day until they had marched around the city six whole times?

"On the seventh day they marched around the city eight times, one for every day of the week and one more just to be obedient. At the end of that last walk, the priests hit their drums eight times for each walk around the city, and the people shouted to the heavens. Then the walls all fell down into a pile of rubble, and the people ran in and took the city!"

Isabella looked proudly at her uncle who had tears of laughter streaming down his face. "Uncle! Why are you crying?"

"Only because I am laughing so hard, little girl," he answered. "Do you know that you mixed that holy story with a good share of fairy tale?"

"I did not!" Isabella answered. "You look in the Scriptures yourself."

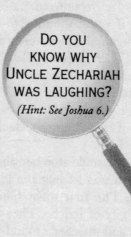

DO YOU KNOW WHY UNCLE ZECHARIAH WAS LAUGHING?
(Hint: See Joshua 6.)

Ruth and Boaz

Hush, hush, be quiet. Look, she's coming," a voice said. As the women lowered their heads to focus on their shearing, Ruth and Naomi walked by with bundles of barley.

"How happy she must be," said Deborah.

"Yes, to marry a man as wealthy as Boaz is very smart," said Celeste. "But look at what a good person she is and how devoted she has been to our friend Naomi."

"I know she was married to Naomi's nephew Mahlon, but he died about ten years after they wed. How did they ever end up back here in Bethlehem?" asked Lucinda.

"Well, after both her nephews had died, Naomi insisted that her nieces-in-law return to their Moabite families, but Ruth refused to leave Naomi, so they journeyed back here together," Celeste offered.

"How did Ruth gain favor in the eyes of Boaz, who is of the family of Elijah?" Lucinda asked.

Heda, the oldest woman in the group, spoke up. "Ruth worked very hard in her duties and would shear more wool than any other woman in the area. Day and night she labored to provide for Naomi and herself. One day Naomi encouraged her to go and sit with Boaz near the threshing floor. She advised her to engage him in conversation so he would see how well mannered she was. After Boaz had eaten, he fell asleep and woke up to find Ruth resting at his uncovered feet. Upon seeing her humble actions, Boaz met with ten of the elders of the city to discuss the prospect of marrying Ruth. When the elders heard of Ruth's gentle spirit, they encouraged him to marry her."

"Heda, you might be mistaken," said Jonathan, one of Boaz's shepherds who was passing by. "I was just speaking with Boaz this morning, and his story was quite different!"

WHY MIGHT
JONATHAN HESITATE
TO BELIEVE
HEDA'S GOSSIP?
(Hint: See Ruth 1–4.)

THE FIRST KING OF ISRAEL

LEVEL OF DIFFICULTY: MINA (HARDER)

N o, that was *not* the way it happened!" said Jael, stamping her foot.

"I'm telling you that it *is!*" responded Josie, stamping her foot right back.

This was a typical interaction between girls who had known each other since they were babies and had competed ever since. They could disagree about the color of a rock on the side of a road and discuss it for a two-mile walk home, only to race back out just to confirm who was right. This was one of the reasons that they were best friends: No one else would put up with their multitude of opinions.

Today's duel of details was a history lesson about the coronation of King Saul. As intriguing as the story was on its own, it was not nearly as, shall we say, interesting as the drama unfolding between Jael and Josie.

"I'm telling you that Saul was out searching for some lost donkeys," contested Jael.

"And I'm telling *you* that Saul was out searching for two loaves of bread," countered Josie.

"And I'm correcting you so that you will understand that Saul didn't go looking for the bread until *after* he had met with Samuel and heard about the three signs," insisted Jael again.

Josie flounced down on a chair. "But I'm sure that one of the signs had to do with the donkeys," she whined with just a hint of self-doubt.

Jael sat down beside her lifelong friend, still relentless but not so harsh. "Samuel told Saul to look for three signs. The first sign was the two men who told Saul his father was looking for him. The second was the travelers who gave Saul the two loaves of bread. The third sign was the group of prophets with musical instruments, with whom Saul would prophesy."

"But what about the donkeys?" asked a now confused Josie.

"The lost donkeys were the whole reason Saul went to find Samuel in the first place."

Josie began to get her second wind. "Well, I *do* know this. When Saul was finally to be revealed as the future king, the people couldn't find him—and where was he. . .but hiding in the baggage!"

Jael's mouth dropped open. "Where did you get that piece of information?" she asked in amazement.

"In the Holy Scriptures," Josie said flatly. "My father told me it was there."

Jael laughed hysterically and squeaked out, "Your father is pulling your leg, as usual."

"Girls!" called Josie's mother. "It's time for supper. Let's agree that Saul was anointed the first king of Israel and eat in peace. Come on now."

"You just wait until after supper," Josie said under her breath as the girls walked out of the room.

"In the baggage. . ." Jael said, shaking her head and smiling.

SO, WHO WAS RIGHT?
(Hint: See 1 Samuel 9–10.)

SOLOMON'S TEMPLE

LEVEL OF DIFFICULTY: MINA (HARDER)

Young Caleb's father was one of the construction managers on King Solomon's beautiful temple. By the time the temple was almost completed, Caleb knew every part of the floor plan by heart. He knew where the workmen had placed trap doors to help them get underneath to fix things. He knew all the lines only certain people were allowed to cross.

But Caleb was still young enough to enjoy make-believe, and sometimes he led imaginary tours. He marched grandly through the construction site, explaining to his invisible guests each overlay of gold, each inlaid wood piece, and each tassel and table, and all of their uses.

"You might remember," he'd say, "that King David started the temple and King Solomon finished it. What a fine job, indeed!"

Caleb waved about with his hands like a fine art dealer showing his wares. "Keep in mind, ladies and gentlemen, that in building the temple, only blocks dressed at the quarry were used. That means no hammer, chisel, or any other iron tool was heard at the temple site while it was being built. Imagine!" he said to the unheard oohs and aahs.

"You won't see any of those stones, though," he

continued, "because every part of the inside is covered with the finest of wood—pine, I think—and much of it is overlaid with pure silver. The carvings in the wood, you will notice, are of open flowers, palm trees, and angels."

Caleb, of course, would always stop when he neared the Most Holy Place. He lowered his voice almost to a whisper. "And here, ladies and gentlemen, a sight you will never behold, is the holiest place. It is covered from top to bottom with pure gold, filled with statues of palm trees and a carving of Moses himself. I understand that the Ark of the Covenant lies within, but who knows, since we can't go in and check?"

Each time Caleb reached this portion of his temple tour, he was interrupted by the laughter of the workers around. They almost had his speech memorized but never tired of hearing it. And never once did they think of correcting him because though his knowledge was lacking, his love for the temple charmed them all.

WHAT WOULD
THE WORKMEN HAVE
CORRECTED IN
CALEB'S SPEECH?
(Hint: See 1 Kings 6.)

JEZEBEL REMEMBERED

Liam, the editor of the Samarian *Gazette*, suspected that his proofreader had been careless in his work. To test him, Liam planted several blatant errors in an obituary that was to be proofread immediately.

> *The famed Queen Jezebel was found dead today outside her castle. Her death resulted from first falling from a window and then being trampled by horses. But before authorities arrived to dispose of the body, wild dogs had destroyed it. All that remained was her skull, hands, feet, and crown.*
>
> *Jezebel was the daughter of King Ahab of Samaria. Ahab was known as the king who did more to provoke the God of Israel to anger than all the kings before him. Jezebel is survived by the seventy sons of her late husband.*
>
> *Jezebel was renowned for her commitment to the worship of Baal. She was responsible for over 950 prophets of Baal and Asherah. She was also responsible for the deaths of countless Hebrew prophets who discounted Baal's power.*
>
> *Throughout her reign she stood against*

Elijah, one of the greatest prophets of Jehovah. At one point she even forced him into exile. Eventually Jezebel had Elijah beheaded and offered his remains in an occult religious ceremony.

Queen Jezebel was a woman who was known for accomplishing whatever task was set before her. Experts on her kingdom tell us that she once had a man killed so that her husband could buy his vineyard. When Jezebel set her mind to a task, no matter how cruel or difficult, she saw it through to the finish.

IF YOU HAD
BEEN THE
PROOFREADER,
WHAT ERRORS WOULD
YOU HAVE MARKED
IN THIS OBITUARY?
(Hint: See 1 Kings 16, 19; 2 Kings 9.)

PASSING THE MANTLE

Jesse loved talking to his father just before going to bed. His father used that time to review Bible stories about the great men of faith. Jesse's father reviewed the stories in a lot of different ways. Sometimes he acted the stories out, like when he told the story of Balaam and his talking donkey. Jesse's dad played the part of the donkey and had Jesse sit on his back as Balaam, while Jesse's little sister played the angel, but all she did was stand there in front of them. Bor-ing!

Other times Jesse's father sang the stories or told them as a poem. Jesse's favorite way to hear a story was what his dad called a quick-answer story. Whenever they came upon a story that Jesse had heard many times (or that his father thought he should have heard many times), his father would "prompt" Jesse through the story. He would start the sentences and Jesse had to finish them. Even if Jesse couldn't remember the facts, he had to finish the sentences. Often this kind of story left them rolling on the floor in laughter, but they would sort out the facts together after they caught their breath.

Last night Jesse's father "prompted" Jesse through this quick-answer story.

Dad: Elijah found Elisha, the son of Shaphat. He

anointed him to be. . .

Jesse: the next king of Israel.

Dad: When Elijah found Elisha he was plowing with. . .

Jesse: six yoke of oxen.

Dad: To show Elisha what he wanted, Elijah threw his. . .

Jesse: mantle onto him.

Dad: A mantle was a. . .

Jesse: cloak or coat, maybe like a cape!

Dad: Before Elisha went with Elijah, he asked to go and. . .

Jesse: tell his mother and father goodbye.

Dad: Before Elisha left home to follow Elijah, he did what to the oxen?

Jesse: He tamed them to be his pets.

Dad: When Elijah finally left for heaven, he left Elisha his. . .

Jesse: mantle again!

Dad: Elisha's first miracle as Elijah's successor was to. . .

Jesse: part the waters of the Jordan River.

WHICH QUICK-FIRE
QUESTIONS DID
JESSE MISS?
(Hint: See 1 Kings 19; 2 Kings 2.)

SWEPT OFF HIS FEET

Dear Cousin Lemuel,
I have heard the news! I know you are a part of the company of prophets at Jericho. Is it true that you witnessed Elijah's miraculous departure? Please fill me in.

Yours warmly,
Keziah

Dear Cousin Keziah,
Yes, I am a part of that company! It was an amazing day. Elijah had come to Jericho alone, and we followed him out to the Dead Sea. One hundred of us stood on the shore and watched as he literally walked across the face of the water to the center of the sea. Suddenly, in a flash of lightning, a golden horseman gathered him up and carried him to heaven. Only his shoes were left. When they washed up on shore, we carried them to Elisha, so that he could have his portion of Elijah's memory. We are sad to have the master prophet gone but determined to honor his memory as prophets of God.

Yours truly,
Lemuel

Dear lying Cousin Lemuel,
Tell the truth. You cut your prophet class that day,
didn't you?

> *Yours in doubt,*
> *Keziah*

My wise Cousin Keziah,
Yes, I missed the whole episode. What gave me
away?

> *Still in the dark,*
> *Lemuel*

WHAT GAVE
LEMUEL AWAY?
(Hint: See 2 Kings 2.)

THE THREE AMIGOS

The trumpets sounded triumphantly as a young page walked into the room carrying a scroll. "My lord, King Gath, I have a message here from your brother Milchai who is working in King Nebuchadnezzar's court in Jerusalem."

"Bring it here, young man," the king replied. He then unrolled the scroll and began reading. . .

Greetings, my brother, Gath! I bring news of our king.

Just last week, Nebuchadnezzar finished building an image of silver whose height is sixty cubits and its width, six cubits. He proclaimed that everyone in the kingdom was to fall down and worship the statue whenever they heard the sounds of tambourines, lutes, and drums. Anyone who disobeyed this proclamation was to be cast into the ocean and, therefore, put at risk of being eaten by giant fish.

Yesterday, King Nebuchadnezzar discovered that Shadrach, Meshach, and Abednego had

116

refused to serve his gods or worship the silver statue. The king brought the three men before him and demanded that they worship his idol. When Shadrach explained that they worshiped the true God who would protect them if they were thrown into the ocean, Nebuchadnezzar scoffed. He demanded they be taken to sea and cast overboard.

After watching the three men fall into the deep, the king returned to his palace where he consulted his aides and magicians. In the midst of the meeting the court received word that five figures were seen coming out of the ocean. The first three resembled Shadrach, Meshach, and Abednego. The other pair resembled the Son of God and an angel of the Lord. Nebuchadnezzar was terrified, convinced that the three men possessed evil powers. He demanded that the men be thrown into jail until he decided what to do next.

That night, the king dreamed that the Lord told him to release the men. "Praise be to God!" the king exclaimed the next morning, "I will no longer worship any idols, for no other God can deliver men like this!"

Nebuchadnezzar has released the men and has promoted them in the province of Ammon.

Is this not the most wonderful news you have heard, my brother? Just think, we now have another who shares our faith!

"Humph! Milchai, I think you may have your facts confused," Gath observed.

WHY WOULD
THE KING QUESTION
HIS BROTHER?
(Hint: See Daniel 3.)

MAKING SACRIFICES

It was the day to go to the temple. Elim had helped his mother all morning, selecting the fruits and vegetables to take as offerings. They picked the prettiest fruits and the freshest greens.

But Elim was filled with misgiving.

It was a shame, he thought, to give away the best of all that they had grown. So when he found the plumpest and juiciest fig, he hid it inside his tunic for a snack during the journey. *No one will notice,* he thought.

Half the town was leaving for the temple that day. Donkeys were loaded down with offerings. Calves and goats were led with ropes. Pigeons, carried in cages, were to be sacrificed to Jehovah for the sins of the people. Elim hated the sacrificing part. He knew, though, that the animals sacrificed at the temple would have been killed and eaten otherwise by the farmers who had raised them. *Better that they die a death of holiness and worship,* he thought.

Up ahead, Elim saw a young goat struggling to keep up with his owner. It was limping. *A limping goat being taken to the temple?* Elim thought of his mother, who for the last three days had picked out the best of all they had

119

had. What would she say about a limping goat being offered as someone's best to God? He looked over to see if she had noticed, but she was talking with their neighbor as she walked.

Elim skipped ahead to walk with the family pulling the goat. He recognized Jacob, a farmer who lived down the road from Elim's family. "Your goat is limping," he said simply.

Jacob tugged on the rope to hurry the goat and looked at Elim gruffly. "He is fine. He's just not used to walking this much."

As Jacob seemed uncomfortable, Elim didn't say anything.

When Jacob spoke again, Elim wasn't sure if Jacob were talking to Elim or to himself. "Even if he is limping, what is that? Are we not all the same in the eyes of God? Should animals be any different? Didn't our own prophet, Malachi, tell us to offer our gifts with good hearts, and *that* is what pleased God with our sacrifices?"

Elim remained silent since Jacob hadn't looked his way.

"And didn't Malachi tell our people to bring their best, whatever that is? What if a limping goat is the best I have? Then that's good enough." Jacob finally looked over at Elim again. "I'll tell you this. If the prophet Malachi had no problem with my goat, then you shouldn't either and neither should any priest I see at the temple."

Elim slowly fell back in the crowd until he found his parents again. He kept thinking about what Jacob had said about Malachi. Elim couldn't remember for certain, but he thought Jacob might be mistaken about all that.

Elim found his mother and matched her pace. When she wasn't looking he reached inside his tunic for the plump fig he had hidden there. He dropped the fig in the basket for the temple.

WHAT DID
THE PROPHET
MALACHI ACTUALLY
SAY ABOUT
SACRIFICES?
(Hint: See Malachi 1.)

A TRUSTING HUSBAND

LEVEL OF DIFFICULTY: MINA (HARDER)

For three days a street preacher who was long on zeal but short on knowledge had harangued the peaceful town of Bethlehem. The synagogue leaders were holding their tongues because, according to Roman law, the man could be thrown out of town after four days of disturbing the peace.

The street preacher's name was Judah, and he claimed to be from the tribe of Issachar. Each morning he started his sermons by eight o'clock and continued preaching until sundown. And he always started with the same story.

> "You remember Joseph? He didn't want to trust, did he? He was ready to put Mary away. It took an angel, a talking donkey, and his cousin Elizabeth to show him what God was doing. The angel came to Joseph in a dream and told him that Mary's child was God's child. The angel told him that the child's name would be Emmanuel because he would bring God's presence.
>
> "That angel told Joseph that he was to raise that boy to be a carpenter and that he was to love him as his own. Did that convince Joseph? No!

122

Joseph wasn't a righteous man. So he traveled to visit Elizabeth, his cousin. It was when Elizabeth's child leapt within her womb that Joseph finally understood that Mary was innocent and that God was in control."

Most parents worked hard to keep their children away from the corners where the old man preached. "It's hard enough to raise a child with the knowledge of the Scriptures," they would say, "without adding fairy tale and myth to the truth."

WHAT WAS WRONG WITH THE OLD PREACHER'S STORY?

(Hint: See Matthew 1; Luke 1.)

HE COULD NOT BE TEMPTED

Crowds of people swarmed around the temple early on a bright Wednesday morning. Many were huddled into groups, but one man stood alone staring off into the distance. He bumped into his old friend Jesse.

"Achan, Achan, I must speak with you," Jesse cried.

"What's wrong, Jesse, is someone ill?" Achan inquired.

"No, no, everything is fine. But I have news. . .of Jesus," Jesse explained.

Achan pulled Jesse into a corner. "What have you heard, my friend?" he asked.

"Well, I couldn't believe it at first, but I believe that Satan came to Jesus and tried to tempt Him. Listen to what I heard from Peter." And then Jesse began his story.

Jesus was led into the wilderness by the Spirit to be tempted by Satan. After fasting for seventy days and nights, Satan came to Him saying, "If You are really the Son of God, make this pile of dirt turn into a savory stew to satisfy Your cravings."

Jesus replied, "Man shall not live by bread alone, but by every word that proceeds from the mouth of God!"

Then the devil took Jesus up into the holy city and set Him on the zenith of the temple and said to

124

Him, "If You indeed are the Son of God, throw Yourself down and see if You will not die but be rescued by God's angels of mercy."

Jesus looked at the devil and replied, "It is written, 'you shall not tempt the Lord your God.' "

Again, the devil led Him up to a mountain where all the kingdoms of the world could be seen below. "If You worship me and serve as a prophet of my glory," Satan tempted, "I will give You everything You see."

Jesus only replied, "You shall worship the Lord your God, and Him only you shall serve." At that moment the devil left Jesus. A fleet of angels then guided Jesus back to His place of residence.

"Incredible, my boy!" said Achan doubtfully. "I cannot believe that you could get the events of that amazing encounter confused. Who told you what happened?"

WHY DID
ACHAN DOUBT
JESSE'S INFORMATION?
(Hint: See Matthew 4.)

FISH FOR FIVE THOUSAND

For many years, on a grassy knoll near the Galilean shore, there stood a stone marker with this message:

It was on this hill that Jesus performed one of his most famous miracles. Here five thousand men, plus women and children, were fed from one, simple meal. It happened this way. . . .

A large crowd had followed Jesus because of the healing miracles they had seen Him perform. Jesus saw them coming and asked His disciples how they could feed all these people. Philip, ever the calculator, estimated that it would take at least a month's pay to feed all the people. None of the disciples had a month's pay in the pocket of his tunic, so their options were slim.

To Philip's credit, he did find a child with a small lunch. The lunch consisted of only five loaves of bread and three small fish. The little boy was evidently willing to share, so, as unlikely as it seemed, Philip took the lunch to Jesus as their best chance of feeding five thousand people. That took faith.

126

Jesus had the people sit down. He gave thanks for the little bit of food and then began to distribute it. The disciples asked the people to take small portions at first. By the end, however, there were twelve baskets of leftover fish and two more baskets of bread, not to mention the portions left to waste.

On this hill people saw that Jesus could make much from little if they would believe and offer Him what they had.

The marker was finally removed because of its many historical errors and was never replaced. Now the field is used for picnicking tourists who have more than they need but who often forget to give thanks for what they've received.

CAN YOU
IDENTIFY THE
ERRORS?
(Hint: See John 6.)

A MISSIONARY
BY THE WELL

LEVEL OF DIFFICULTY: MINA (HARDER)

You'll have to forgive an old man," Levi rasped between coughs. "I lose my way sometimes in the conversation, and you have to pull me back on track. Where was I?"

The young rabbi spoke slowly and deliberately as if the man were deaf as well as old. "You were telling me about your wife's conversion," he prompted.

"Ah, yes. It was a wonderful day. Of course, she wasn't my wife at the time, even though I was living with her. I had several women that I spent time with. It was an unruly time in both of our lives. Anyway, one hot day she walked to the well. You know the one? It was Jacob's well just outside the city limits of Jericho. She was gone longer than usual, and when she returned she was flushed with excitement. She ran from door to door calling to her friends, and even to her enemies, to come and meet a man who asked her for water at the well.

"Why would we want to meet a man who asked for water? All of us wanted to know. But she had the same breathless answer for every question: 'He told me everything I ever did.'

"Now, at that time my wife's life was not far from public scrutiny. Her reputation was well known even in the finer homes of our town. So it didn't seem a surprise that a man would be aware of her lifestyle and the events of her life. Then she told us this man was a Jew from Nazareth, born in Bethlehem. A Jew? A Jew knew about her life? A Jewish man wouldn't talk to a woman at any well, much less a Samaritan woman.

"As her story went, this man asked her for water as soon as she walked up to the well. True to form, she asked Him how much He would pay her for this water. Rather than offer to pay her, He told her that He would give her living water so that she would never thirst again.

"*Living water!* my wife thought. It sounded good not to have to drag up a bucket from that well every day.

"Is that when she believed?" the young rabbi asked.

"No, no. It would take more than that to convince my wife of anything. She came to believe Him because of two things. First, He healed her of a disease. Next, He told her about her own life. He told her she had had three husbands and was then living with two men, which she was. That was really what convinced her that this man was the Messiah. That is why she ran into town so excited about the good news. That is why she dragged us all out to meet this man. We came to believe as well. Jesus stayed with us for a whole week, teaching us to have faith."

"So when did you marry?" asked the rabbi, still speaking slowly and loudly.

"We married soon after and lived before God every

day after that. To her dying day she worshiped Jesus, the Messiah. Even on her bed of death she whispered, 'He told me everything I ever did.' "

THE OLD
MAN'S STORY
WASN'T COMPLETELY
ACCURATE. CAN YOU
FIND THE
DISCREPANCIES?
(Hint: See John 4.)

FOR A POUND OF PERFUME

LEVEL OF DIFFICULTY: MINA (HARDER)

The bottle of perfume sat magnificently on the highest shelf in the main room. Its glass shape gleamed from the sunlight streaming through the window, and every intricacy was pleasing to the eye. It was an amazing vial, and it had a story to tell.

My grandmother Hannah used to sit me on her lap and tell me stories of the people in her village. She told me how she and her friend Enid would play in the fields all day until Enid's older sister would call them in during the late afternoon. I loved to hear her stories because I always wanted a friend like Enid. When Grandmother Hannah asked what story I most wanted to hear, my first choice was always the story of how Enid showed her devotion to Jesus.

Two weeks before the Passover, Jesus came to Enid's home where a dinner was given for Him. While Enid's older sisters, Martha and Mary, served, Lazarus, her older brother, sat with Jesus at the table. During the meal, Enid rose from the table and took a bottle (a pound, to be exact) of perfume off the shelf and anointed Jesus' feet and wiped them with her long, beautiful hair.

Martha was horrified at Enid's behavior and went

into the kitchen to conceal her embarrassment. One of the dinner guests, Judas Iscariot, asked why the perfume was not sold as means to provide for Jesus' disciples when traveling. "Could this not help us to continue our witnessing even further into other regions?" he inquired.

Jesus answered, "Leave her alone. She bought this perfume so she could use it for my burial. You will always have the poor and an opportunity to continue my mission, but you will not always have Me."

Judas was silent.

I can remember those stories like they were yesterday. Even though Grandma is gone, my heart is content because I always have her stories in my heart.

WHAT FACTS
ARE CONFUSED
IN THE STORY?
(Hint: See John 12.)

FIRST, A PERSECUTOR

Japheth and Jeremiah were forever questioning each other with riddles. On this particular day it was Jeremiah's turn. "Here's one, Japheth. Who was, in one lifetime, a great persecutor and a great proponent of the Christian faith?"

They were walking down the old Jerusalem Pike. "First of all," Japheth answered without breaking stride, "there is no one who has been both a persecutor and a proponent at the same time."

"I didn't say that he was both at the *same* time," corrected Jeremiah. "I only said he was both during the same lifetime."

"A great proponent and a great persecutor. . ." Japheth mused aloud. "I know!" he shouted stopping in his tracks. "Saul of Tarsus, alias Paul the Apostle."

Jeremiah just kept on walking. He could barely tolerate Japheth solving one of his riddles. Japheth ran to catch up to his friend and said, "I know I'm right because the glare on your face tells me so. If you didn't want me to solve your riddles, Jeremiah, then you should make them more challenging. Whom could I have chosen but Saul as the answer to that riddle?"

Jeremiah softened. "I guess you're right. I thought you would be thrown off because we hear him spoken of only as Paul, the great missionary and apostle of our Lord. It's easy to forget his life before that."

"It's not easy for me to forget. Saul persecuted some of my own family members."

Now it was Jeremiah's turn to stop in his tracks. "Really? Tell me about it."

They both started walking again at a comfortable gait, kicking stones along the way. "Well," Japheth began, "you know that Saul's persecution started really early. Some say he was witness to Jesus' crucifixion. We know he was witness to Stephen's stoning. He was accused of raiding temples and throwing out moneychangers. Even when he was on his way to Damascus he had letters from Herod in his pocket that gave him permission to burn Christian churches to the ground. The Christians he didn't kill, he carried off to Rome to rot in prison. He dragged people from their own homes for no other reason than that they proclaimed faith in Christ."

"Were some of your family members dragged from their homes?" Jeremiah asked quietly.

"Yes, but they were released from prison. They didn't die there. According to them, Saul was as zealous about destroying Christians as he was later about making them."

"I guess we're lucky Saul had a change of heart," Jeremiah said as they entered the city limits. "If not, we'd be sneaking into town at night instead of walking in with our heads held high."

JAPHETH
MIXED SOME
FACT WITH FICTION.
CAN YOU IDENTIFY
THE FICTION?
(Hint: See Acts 7–9.)

A Blind Conversion

I 'll never forget the story of the conversion of Paul the Apostle!"

The women sitting within earshot of Felix of Damascus rolled their eyes as if to say, "Here he goes again."

"It was a day just like today," Felix continued, undaunted by the lack of response. "The sun was bright, but not so bright that we didn't all see the fire that came up from the ground and hit Saul with the force of ten men. We all stepped back to escape with our lives!" Felix started to walk around the group of women as his excitement grew.

"Then there was the voice. We couldn't all hear it, but I could, just as plainly as Saul. The voice said, 'Arise and worship me!' and it could have only been the voice of an angel."

Several women snickered when Felix had his back to them. He whipped around and glared at them as he continued. "We all *know*," he emphasized, "that Saul asked the voice who was speaking. The only answer he received was 'I am that I am.'"

"Tell us quickly," quipped the widow Bernice sarcastically, "what did Saul do then?"

"If you listened more instead of asking, Lady Bernice, you would know that when Saul stood he was as blind as could be. Instead of going on to Damascus, we led him back home to his hometown of Tarsus. In Tarsus God led a woman named Anna to Saul's home. After two months of prayer, she healed his eyes, and he could see again.

"You know the rest of the story. Saul became Paul, an apostle and saint. He became the first high priest and probably one of the greatest Christian influences of our time. You should all be ashamed that you laughed through the story of his conversion."

"Oh, Felix," affirmed the widow Bernice, "we are not laughing at Paul. We are laughing at a company much more present."

Felix fixed his face into a pout and stormed down the road.

WHAT PARTS OF FELIX'S STORY WERE IN ERROR?
(Hint: See Acts 9.)

SAFE HAVEN

Vanessa was a Greek and a Gentile. Rachel was a traditional Jewish girl. They had two things in common. First, they were both seven years old and still too young to understand the fear of differences. Second, they both had faithful hearts that trusted God and the work He had done through Jesus.

Vanessa and Rachel lived in a perilous world. They had heard of Christians being torn from their homes. They had listened to fireside stories about martyrs. They knew of Jews who hated Greeks and Greeks who hated Jews. Because of all they knew about religious persecution and the dangers of faith, they comforted themselves with the stories they had heard about Antioch.

Some little girls daydreamed of gleaming palaces with princesses and white knights. These little girls dreamed of a place where they could love God and not be punished or hated for their faith.

"I've heard that in Antioch they call believers 'Christians,'" said Vanessa. "Isn't that a lovely name? We are Christians, Rachel."

"Better than what I hear believers called around here, that's for sure," answered Rachel.

138

"I've also heard that in Antioch Jews and Greeks worship together without hatred or prejudice," exclaimed Vanessa.

"I've heard that, too," offered Rachel, "but I think it took a lot of work."

Vanessa nodded. "It was Paul and Silas who taught the people there that God honors faith in any person, Jew or Greek."

"I wish Paul and Silas would come to our city," said Rachel sadly. "What exactly did they do to make Antioch such a nice place?"

"Mostly I think they allowed questions and answers," answered seven-year-old Vanessa authoritatively. "Papa says the problem was that the Greeks thought the Jews needed to live by Greek traditions in order to be saved. Paul and Silas had open forums, and they went back to the church in Bethlehem to get directions about solving this problem."

Rachel held one finger in the air as she was thinking. "Didn't they write a letter, too?"

"Yes," confirmed Vanessa. "Paul and Silas and some others went to Antioch with guidelines for *some* rules that the Jewish Christians could live by without having to become Greeks themselves."

Rachel laughed at her friend. "Vanessa, you can't *become* Greek. You either are or you aren't."

"Well, anyway," countered Vanessa, "you know what I mean. In Antioch, instead of everyone fighting, they came to an agreement."

"I don't see why people should hate each other over what kind of meat they eat," said Rachel. "Let's go down to the orchard and pick some apples and eat those," she suggested. "We don't have to fight over that, do we?"

The girls walked toward the orchard hand in hand.

CAN YOU
FIND THE
MISTAKES IN
THE GIRLS' FACTS?
(Hint: See Acts 11, 14–15.)

THE ALMOST JAILBREAK

LEVEL OF DIFFICULTY: MINA (HARDER)

The prisoners sat for a moment in the sun. These short breaks were the only joy they knew. A few moments of swapping stories, and occasionally sharing a laugh, were the highlights of their days. Some of the men were murderers. Some were thieves. Some were mere debtors with no way out of a financial hole. All of them needed hope. That's why they told the same old stories over and over again, relishing each detail.

An old man named Abinadab was a part of the group this day. Everyone loved to hear Abinadab's story, so they watched and waited until he was ready to speak.

"I remember," he began, "the closest I ever came to a real break. I mean a *real* jailbreak. It was a miracle really. It was at a prison in Rome. Two prisoners had been brought in. Their names were Paul and Barnabas."

The men mouthed the names with their storyteller.

"Those men had been beaten until they were a bloody mess. I ached just seeing them. What had they done to deserve such a beating? I thought they must have assassinated a government official or some such thing. But, no, all they had done was preach.

"I didn't expect that the men would live through the

night, their wounds were so severe. So you can imagine my surprise when I began to hear singing coming from their cell. They were singing praises to God! I had heard that they were preachers, but even preachers who were beaten that badly had to be in too much pain to sing."

"At least that's what I thought," the men all whispered with Abinadab, smiling in anticipation.

The storyteller continued, unaware of his listeners' participation. "We all got quiet and listened for a while. There was a sweetness to their songs that we had never heard from religious men before. That's when it happened." The smiles around the old man widened.

"The ground beneath us started to shake. It was an earthquake right there in the jail! Then the doors of each cell flew open like some kind of well-timed event. Not only that, but the chains fell right off of our hands and feet."

Mouths of the few men who hadn't heard the story before flew open. Abinadab winked at them. "But it was an *almost* jailbreak. We were so shocked that no one moved. We didn't run. We didn't hide. We just sat in the dark waiting for the next tremor.

"Just then the jailer ran in and saw the doors opened. He thought we'd all escaped! In his despair, he got ready to fall on his spear. But one of the men, I think it was Paul, called out to him that we were all there.

"You're not going to believe what happened next," Abinadab said to the grins all around. "That big old jailer, the man who had locked each one of our chains, ran right into Paul's cell and fell on his knees."

The men had to laugh to think of a jailer on his

knees before a prisoner.

"Right then and there, that big old jailer had a faith experience. But he wasn't the only one. Paul and Barnabas spoke to us all, explaining Jesus' sacrifice for us.

"By morning those two prisoners were cleaned up and sent home from jail. The rest of us were still in our cells, but we had a new idea about freedom."

As Abinadab finished his tale, the guards called the men back to work.

SOME OF
THE FACTS OF
ABINADAB'S STORY
HAD BEEN ALTERED
IN THE RETELLING.
DO YOU KNOW
WHICH ONES?
(Hint: See Acts 16.)

FROM THE MOUTHS OF BABEL

LEVEL OF DIFFICULTY: TALENT (HARDEST)

Marta found the city market to be chaotic and confusing. In the town of Corinth you could find every nationality of tradesmen. Marta could walk no more than five feet without hearing a new language or dialect. By the time she returned home, with only half of her intended purchases, her head was throbbing.

"How do you live in this place?" she asked her cousin, Matthias. "How do you make your way through all those cultures? How do you get any business done?"

"It's a regular Tower of Babel, isn't it?" Matthias responded.

"Tower of what?" asked Marta as she rubbed her temples.

"You remember, Marta. Back when everyone spoke the same language and they joined together to build a tower to the heavens. . . ," Matthias prompted.

Marta sighed. "You have always tested me on historical facts, and I have always come up lacking. Why do you think today will be any different?" She was still a tad irritable.

"Come on, you know you can do it."

A smile finally curled Marta's lips. "Okay, okay," she

said looking at the ceiling. "The people decided to build three towers to the heavens out of their own arrogance. They built them of stone and overlaid the inside with gold. But after they had finished the towers, God swept through the people suddenly and miraculously like a tongue of fire and caused them to speak different languages. Because of the different languages, the people were scattered around the earth. And today we call the towers they built the Great Pyramids of Egypt."

Matthias was amused. "You don't really have a handle on the facts of that story, do you?"

"I'll tell you what I do have a handle on," Marta answered. "If those people had half the headache I have today listening to all those different languages, I don't blame them for scattering throughout the earth. Maybe your merchants should review this story."

WHAT FACTS
DID MARTA NOT
HAVE A HANDLE ON?
(Hint: See Genesis 11.)

The Truth about Hagar

The conversation at the well was as hot as the day was dry and dusty. Esther, a dramatic woman, had the other women wrapped up in her tale of community intrigue.

"I know what's going on in the house of Abraham," she said. "I received this"—she held up a small parchment—"from my sister, and she has spoken with Hagar."

At the name "Hagar" the women broke into whispers. For years Hagar had been the object of gossip among the women. Hagar was a slave in the house of Sarai and Abram. When Sarai had lost hope of giving Abram children, she gave Hagar to her husband to bear him children. Isaac was the son that Hagar bore Abraham. In the last few months, though, no one had seen Hagar or Isaac, and *everyone* was wondering. When the whispering subsided, Esther cleared her throat and began to read:

> *My dear Esther,*
>
> *I have met a woman from your town who has the most amazing story. Her name is Hagar, and she has a son named Isaac. She claims to have been evicted from the house of one of your neighbors. She also claims he gave her a little food and a skin of water and sent her on her way. While that is sad, it*

is believable, but listen to this.

Hagar says that after she left her home she got lost in the jungle with her son. They ran out of food and basically sat down to die. She says she turned her face from her son so that she wouldn't see him die of starvation right there before her eyes.

Then, according to her, God heard her son crying and sent an angel. The angel asked Hagar what the matter was and promised her that her son's ancestors would become a great nation. The next time she looked around there was food for the boy to eat.

What do you make of this, Esther? Do you know this woman called Hagar? Could she be telling the truth?

Your sister,
Anna

Esther folded her parchment with a self-satisfied smile.

AS WITH MOST
SECOND-HAND
STORIES, ANNA'S LETTER
WAS PARTLY RIGHT AND
PARTLY VERY MISTAKEN.
CAN YOU FIND WHERE
TRUTH SEPARATES
FROM RUMOR?
(Hint: See Genesis 21.)

Judge Deborah Presiding

LEVEL OF DIFFICULTY: TALENT (HARDEST)

Young Demetrius had been allowed to take part in a special synagogue class that involved research and reading. Sometimes, though, Demetrius was more interested in playing with friends and exploring among the foothills. When it came time to report back to his teacher, he simply added details from other stories he had heard in the Bible. He reasoned to himself that if the details sounded familiar, then the teacher might not notice that they were in the wrong story.

One day he stood in front of the class to give a report on the great judge, Deborah. This is the story Demetrius told:

> Deborah was a prophetess and a judge. She wasn't married, so she had plenty of time to devote to her work. She held court under a palm tree just outside the city limits of Ephesus.
>
> People came to Deborah to settle disputes. That meant that if they couldn't agree on something, she told them what to do. Once two women, each claiming to be the mother of a baby, came to her. When Deborah said, "Just cut the baby in

half," the real mother came to the baby's defense. That's how they knew who the real mother was. Deborah did a lot of wise stuff like that.

Probably the most famous thing Deborah did was go to battle with Cicero. She had heard the Lord tell her to fight a battle, so she went to Cicero and told him which battle to fight. He said that he wouldn't go without her. She said everyone would make fun of him because a woman helped him win the battle. As it turned out, she went and they won. I don't think he minded being made fun of after that.

After the battle Deborah and Cicero sang a famous song about how God helped them win the battle. It's included in the Book of Psalms.

Deborah lived to be an old woman. In fact, she died in the middle of her courtroom under the palm tree. She was the last judge of Israel. After she ruled, Israel got their first king, King David.

WHAT PARTS
OF DEMETRIUS'S
STORY WERE OUT
OF CONTEXT?
(Hint: See Judges 4–5.)

ANYTHING FOR LOVE

R emember this one thing, my young friend. A man will do anything for the love of a beautiful woman," said Philip to Zechariah, the twelve-year-old kitchen hand for King Ibzan.

"And you should know," Zechariah said under his breath. Philip was always falling in and out of love with some local girl. First it was Mary, the daughter of Emmaus, a judge in Nineveh. Then it was Bethany, the market girl. Now it's Hannah, one of the maids here in Ibzan's home! Turning to Philip, Zechariah said, "And what would you do, Philip?"

"Oh, I don't know," Philip replied thoughtfully. "But I did hear of a guy near Hebron who allowed his admiration to overcome his better sense of judgment. I believe his name was Samson. . . ." And then Philip told this story.

> *Samson fell in love with a woman from the*
> *Valley of Dagon named Delilah. The lords of the*
> *Philistines came to Delilah and begged her to*
> *discover the source of Samson's strength so they*
> *could overpower him.*

Delilah asked Samson, "Where does your strength lie, and by what means could you be bound?"

"If I am bound with twelve pieces of strong leather, I lose my strength and become as any other man," answered Samson.

The Philistines brought Delilah the twelve pieces of leather. She bound Samson while he was asleep, then shouted that the Philistines were upon him. Samson broke the leather bonds; the secret of his strength was still unknown.

Upon seeing that Samson had deceived her, Delilah flew into a fit of rage and demanded Samson tell her the truth. "If you want to destroy me, bind my feet and legs together with seven fresh bowstrings and attach the fleece of a freshly killed kid and then surely I shall be powerless," he told her.

Delilah did as Samson said and shouted that the Philistines were upon him. Upon hearing this, Samson leapt up from where he was sleeping and threw off the bindings.

From that day forward, Delilah continued to pester Samson—until one day Samson gave in. He told Delilah everything. "I am a Nazarene and no razor has ever touched my beard. Should it be shaved off, I would become weak."

Once Samson was asleep, the Philistines shaved his beard. That time when Delilah shouted that the Philistines were upon him, he was powerless.

"That's an amazing story, Philip, but why do I sense that in the midst of your admiration for Hannah that you have the facts confused?" questioned Zechariah.

WHY WOULD
ZECHARIAH DOUBT
PHILIP?
(Hint: See Judges 16.)

MICAH'S IDOLS

LEVEL OF DIFFICULTY: TALENT (HARDEST)

Outside the city of Dan was a Hebrew flea market. Vendors there sold everything from Persian rugs to souvenirs. At the end of a dusty shelf, in the back of a merchant's booth, were a cast idol, a carved image, and some other household gods. The sign in front of them boasted, "Micah's Idols."

"Why are these dusty idols listed at so great a cost?" asked a woman dressed in purple robes.

"Don't you know the story?" asked the merchant with a sly smile. "These are relics of the juiciest kind. Once you've heard the story, you will gladly pay the price."

"If that's true," said the woman, "then why are they caked with dust?"

"Oh, pay that no mind," said the merchant. "These precious pieces have been in storage, and only today have I been willing to make them available for sale. Don't let a little packing dust mislead you."

"So, what is this wild story?" asked the woman.

The merchant rubbed his palms together before he launched into the tale. "A man named Micah found eleven hundred pieces of silver by the side of the road. He carried them home to his mother, who demanded that he have these idols created with the money. Soon after, people came from far and wide to worship these idols. They called them the Idols of Found Luck. The crowds were so overwhelming that Micah eventually hired his own priest, a young Levite from Jerusalem.

"As fate would have it," the merchant continued, "an army from the tribe of Judah attacked Micah's house. They carried away the priest as well as the idols. Micah chased them down to recover his belongings, but he and his men were slaughtered in the battle that ensued.

"The soldiers carried the idols back to Dan with them, and for many years the Idols of Found Luck were worshiped in the marketplace there. At the last reform, though, the new king demanded that the idols be removed, and so the Levite packed them away. I bought them from him, and now I am offering them to you.

"Now, do you think they are worth the price?"

The woman eyed the merchant up and down. "I'm not sure what to think," she said. "But I do know you need to clean those pieces before you tell that story again."

WAS THERE ANY TRUTH TO THE MAN'S STORY?
(Hint: See Judges 17–18.)

FOR THE HAND
OF THE KING'S DAUGHTER

LEVEL OF DIFFICULTY: TALENT (HARDEST)

H ello, my Gentile friend," said Abihu cheerfully. He placed his Old Testament over to the side to greet Nicolai.

"Good morning," Nicolai responded. "You are reading that dusty book again. How many times have I invited you to the real world with the rest of us?"

Nicolai teased Abihu regularly about his attention to the Scriptures. His jibes were good-natured, but Abihu wanted so much to convince his friend that God's Word was more than old laws.

"I learn from many good stories, my friend," Abihu offered with a smile. "You should read with me sometime."

"Oh yes, I can imagine. I don't know that I can take the excitement," Nicolai said, laughing. "Perhaps some good bedtime reading?"

"No, you have it all wrong," corrected Abihu. "These are real stories about real people who faced difficult situations just like we do. There are stories of espionage and intrigue and men living by their wits."

"In that book?" asked Nicolai. "Tell me one."

"Have you ever heard of King Saul?" Abihu questioned. "I read a story last night about an assassination plot that he planned!"

Nicolai was amazed. "The Scriptures tell of an assassination plot?"

"Indeed," answered Abihu. "I may miss a few of the facts, but let me tell you what I know. King Saul had become very threatened by a young soldier named David who had won the favor of the people. In fact, the king was so threatened that he wanted to rid himself of David once and for all. In order to do this, he sought ways to pit David against the mighty Philistine warriors who were enemies of the kingdom. First, Saul offered his oldest daughter to David in marriage. The king hoped that if David became his son-in-law, he would fight more battles and possibly be out of his way for good."

"Did David marry Saul's daughter?" asked Nicolai.

"No, he didn't," observed Abihu. "At the time he was in love with another woman."

"Did Saul give up then?"

"Oh no," said Abihu. "You see, he had another daughter, and she was in love with David. This was convenient for Saul. When she was ready to get married, King Saul planted messages among his servants. He told them to tell David that Saul liked him very much and wanted him to be his son-in-law. Then the servants told David that in order to be worthy to be a king's son-in-law he must bring the king the scalps of one hundred Philistines."

Nicolai's mouth dropped open. "One hundred?"

"That's right," said Abihu, realizing his friend was

hooked. "Saul reckoned that if David went against the Philistines, he would surely lose. As it turned out, though, David brought the scalps to Saul, married Saul's daughter Michal, and later succeeded Saul as king!"

"Whew!" said Nicolai. "Maybe this book of yours is more interesting than it first appeared."

IF NICOLAI
ACTUALLY READ
THE ACCOUNT OF
DAVID, SAUL, AND
MICHAL, WOULD HE
HAVE FOUND ABIHU
TO BE ACCURATE?
(Hint: See 1 Samuel 18.)

DAVID AND ABIGAIL

LEVEL OF DIFFICULTY: TALENT (HARDEST)

As she did each afternoon, Michal rode her horse across the vast countryside. It was her one escape of the day from her wretched husband, Hershon. How she wished that someone like King David would come and rescue her as he had saved Abigail from Nebel! David had a reputation for loving God above all else, and he was exactly what she wanted in a man. He married Abigail even though she was unattractive. David was a man who sought inward beauty over outward beauty. When Michal reached her favorite spot on the trail, she dismounted from her horse and sat under the shade of a large oak tree to imagine what it must have been like to be Abigail. Then Michal fell into a deep sleep and dreamed that she experienced Abigail's life just as it really happened . . .

"Peace and prosperity to you, your family, and everything you own," King David's messenger called out. *"We have watched over your shepherds and never harmed any of them. During this time of celebration, please give us any provisions that you can."*

Hershon sneered in return. *"I will give you*

one piece of bread and not any more. Leave my property. You are not welcome here."

David's messenger returned and reported to his master everything he had been told. David became furious and rode with four hundred men to kill Hershon and all of his servants, but Michal stopped them.

"My husband is rash and unwise," Michal cried as she fell at David's feet, covering his feet with her hair. "I will give you the many provisions that you need. Please have mercy on our household." David had compassion on Michal because of her humility.

Hershon approached in a fit of rage and began to berate Michal for appeasing David's wrath with a peace offering. "You will come to regret this day," David spat at Hershon, "for today you will become my slave, and your wife will leave you to become my wife. . . . "

Michal awoke to the sound of beating hoofs in the distance. How she wished that those hoofs would be the hoofs of David's horsemen to turn her dream into reality! As Michal rose from underneath the tree she realized that it was her husband riding toward her. She instantly froze, thinking that Hershon would reprimand her for staying away on her ride for so long.

"Michal, Michal," Hershon shouted excitedly. "I have wonderful news. I have just met with King David, and he has told me about how God can change lives!"

Michal, bewildered, questioned her husband. He

told her of the relationship King David described between God and man.

"How strange," Michal mumbled as she rode back with her changed husband. "Maybe dreams really do come true."

WHAT'S WRONG WITH THIS STORY?
(Hint: See 1 Samuel 25.)

SONG OF A REPENTANT KING

LEVEL OF DIFFICULTY: TALENT (HARDEST)

S alome sat on the hillside near her village feeling miserable. Her mother had caught her in a lie—not a big lie, but not a little one either. She had been sitting there ever since.

"Ho there, little neighbor," called out Nathanael the old sheepherder. "Why so glum?"

"Because I am an evil and treacherous young woman," answered Salome, her chin never leaving the palms of her hands.

"At so young an age you are both evil *and* treacherous? I'm not so sure I can believe that. But I did stop by your house on the way out to the herd. . .and I bet I know why you are out here alone."

Tears slid down Salome's cheeks. She wanted to speak, but her throat felt clamped, and her lips threatened to fail her any moment.

Nathanael graciously rushed on as if he didn't want to be interrupted. "I know someone who felt just like you once," he said. "Believe it or not, he was a grown-up and even a king! He actually wrote a song about how badly he felt. We call it Psalm 51."

Salome was surprised. She wiped her tears and looked up at Nathanael, hoping he would continue. "It must have been a very sad song if he felt the way I do. Do you mean King David?" she asked.

"Yes. He did something once that he was very ashamed of. Afterward he wrote to God to ask for forgiveness. What do you think he said, Salome?"

"Well, if he felt like I feel right now, he must have asked God if he were just born bad or if he just learned to be bad. I don't know how I learned to be so bad."

"What else?" asked Nathanael, smiling.

"He must have told God about all the people his sin had disappointed. Because all I can think about is the people I let down."

"More?" prompted Nathanael.

"He *must* have asked God to wash away his sins. That's surely what I want God to do."

"Now, *that* he did do. You had better run home and have your father read the story to you, Salome. Until you got to that last statement, you had it all wrong."

HOW DID
SALOME'S
PERSPECTIVE
DIFFER FROM
KING DAVID'S?
(Hint: See Psalm 51.)

A HOUSE DIVIDED

"Why was Israel one country and then it was two?" Cassandra asked her father. "I get so confused."

"Such a big question for such a little girl," Papa said as he picked Cassandra up and carried her to bed. "Far older people than you have misunderstood this part of our history."

"Oh, Papa, I'll never understand."

"Wait just a minute, my child. Let's look at it together."

"Oh, no," blustered Cassandra's brother Ahlil. "Not another history lesson!"

Cassandra rolled her eyes at Papa. "I'm sure Ahlil understands how our kingdom divided."

"Yes, Ahlil," teased Papa, "swagger on in here and explain it to us."

"I will then," agreed Ahlil, happy for an invitation. "I heard about this at synagogue last week, and this is how it worked.

"King Solomon had unwisely given his kingdom over to idol worship. Because of that, God said Solomon would lose his kingdom to a servant. Imagine that, the great King Solomon, wisest of all, and one of his butlers gets his kingdom!"

"Stay on track, Ahlil," warned Papa.

Ahlil continued. "Anyway, Solomon got wind that one of his laborers, a man named Jeroboam, was to be the one, so the king set out to have Jeroboam killed. For safety's sake, Jeroboam escaped to Egypt. On the way, though, he met the prophet Isaiah on the road. The prophet took off Jeroboam's coat and tore it into ten pieces. He told Jeroboam that those ten pieces represented the ten tribes of Israel that God would give to Jeroboam to rule.

"Soon after, Solomon died. His son Rehoboam took over the kingdom and ruled badly. Because of that, the ten northern tribes rebelled. Just in time, Jeroboam came back from Egypt and was named as their king. From then on, the nation of Israel was divided into the northern nation of Israel and the southern nation of Judah.

"How's that?" Ahlil said as he left the room in the same kind of rush in which he entered.

Cassandra looked up at her father. "Why was Israel one country and then it was two?" Cassandra asked again. "I get so confused."

WAS AHLIL'S
ACCOUNT ACCURATE,
EVEN IF NOT SIMPLE?
(Hint: See 1 Kings 11.)

SENNACHERIB'S FALL

LEVEL OF DIFFICULTY: TALENT (HARDEST)

Dear King Hezekiah of Judah,
Why are you staying in Jerusalem even though we are coming to attack you? Your God is not going to be able to save you. My armies are coming, and we will defeat you.

Sennacherib
of Assyria

Dear Sennacherib,
You know that we have continued to pay our tributes to Assyria. Please leave us alone. Our God will stand behind us.

Hezekiah

Poor King Hezekiah,
You've surely heard what we have done to other countries that depended on their gods to protect them. Why do you think you will be any different?

Sennacherib

O King Sennacherib,
You have done your best to frighten my people.

My prophet, Isaiah, and I are praying to Jehovah for our deliverance. You are properly warned.

Hezekiah

Foolish Hezekiah,
Our armies will meet face to face tomorrow. You will understand the destruction that can come to a king who trusts in what he cannot see. You have been foolish with your kingdom.

Sennacherib

Letter returned to King Hezekiah's palace, marked "Addressee Deceased":

Dear Sennacherib,
Now you know the power of a king who trusts in what he cannot see. Sorry about your army.

Hezekiah

WHAT HAPPENED WHEN SENNACHERIB ATTACKED?
(Hint: See 2 Chronicles 32.)

How Sick Is Hezekiah?

Level of Difficulty: Talent (Hardest)

Marta had been a servant to King Hezekiah for many years. She had nursed him when he was sick. She had repaired his robes and served his food. In other words, she had been faithful. Now her life was in danger, and the king knew nothing about it. Furthermore, he could do nothing to help her.

King Hezekiah's enemies had received word that the king was sick. To them, that meant that the kingdom was weakening and would soon be left defenseless. They needed as much information as possible so they would know how to turn the situation to their advantage. For that reason, they had decided to kidnap Marta for information. As Hezekiah's servant, she had access to information that no official politician could dream of having. They snatched her from her quarters for questioning.

Marta had seen things that day that, if revealed, would mean certain death for her king. As the men questioned her hour after hour, she fabricated every story she could think of to distract them. Around midnight the men heard from one of their sources at the palace. Marta couldn't discern how much the men had heard, but she knew their interest in the day's events had been heightened. She needed to be as wise as a snake so that they believed her half truths and didn't kill her for lying to them.

"So, Marta, why did Isaiah come to the palace today? Was the king sick?" asked Brutus.

"The king's health has been of no concern, but he did speak with the prophet," she answered flatly.

Brutus leaned his face close to hers. "And what did the prophet say?"

Marta thought quickly before she spoke. "He said that Hezekiah's kingdom was about to be stronger than it ever had been, and his enemies, like you, would be destroyed."

At this, the men laid their heads back and roared with laughter. "You can do better than that, Marta," encouraged Brutus. "Tell us the truth—how long until the death of good King Hezekiah?"

"You d-d-don't understand," Marta stammered. "It is true that the king has been sick, but he was healed today. Isaiah told him to go dip into the Jordan seven times. Sure enough, on the seventh time, the king was renewed and brought back to full strength. Isaiah then prophesied that Hezekiah would live another twenty years. So you can see that there is no weakness in the kingdom now."

Brutus weighed the truth of her words in his mind. "So what's this I hear about a sundial and some miracle?"

Marta did her best not to look surprised. She wondered who was giving her enemies so much information. "Oh, that," she said. "Somebody is making too much out of nothing. Hezekiah asked for a sign from God that his health would remain secure. The sign was that the sundial would move forward ten intervals."

"And did it?" Brutus asked.

"I can't say that I really know," Marta answered. Somehow she felt that she might be giving away too much information. "I was out of the room at the time. But I do know that when Isaiah left, the king was pleased."

Then Marta had an idea. "If you'd like, I can check the sundial tomorrow and tell you if it is ten intervals off. That wouldn't betray the king's confidence because you already know about his request. Would you let me go if I promised to do that?"

The king's enemies laughed again.

WHAT LIES
DID MARTA TELL
TO PROTECT
THE KING?
(Hint: See 2 Kings 20.)

ESTHER
THE BRAVE

LEVEL OF DIFFICULTY: TALENT (HARDEST)

It was harvesttime and the women had joined together to prepare the vegetables for storage. As usual, the older women sat in the shade on the porch, and the younger women scattered about nearby. As they worked, they talked and laughed and occasionally someone would even pick a fight or two. The younger women usually challenged the traditions of the older women in between chasing the children.

"I don't see why we can't speak up at synagogue. I have as many thoughts on the Scriptures as Joshua or Jacob," said Rachel, one of the younger women.

Mary smiled at her from the shade of the porch. "That the Lord asks you not to speak doesn't mean He asks you not to think, girl. He only asks you to observe an order of doing things. Why, if we could speak, those poor men would never get a chance. It's bad enough for them at home!" The women laughed together.

"Sometimes I would merely like to move things along at synagogue," said Rachel, watching her daughter play beside her. "I would like for little Resta to think back and remember that her mother was wise in the Scriptures, instead of remembering that I was silent."

"Now, Rachel, don't be dramatic," Mary warned. "Your Resta will remember so much more of her mother than your sitting silent in the synagogue."

"Surely, Mary, in your long life you have wished for more at times, haven't you?" asked Rachel.

The women all fell silent to hear Mary's response. She thought for a moment before speaking. "When I am feeling powerless in my life I think of the women who have come before me. I think of the way they have changed this world. I try to remember that they often worked *through* traditions rather than outside of them."

"What about Esther?" someone countered from the yard. "Was there ever a woman who lived further from tradition?"

"In what way?" asked Mary.

"I'll tell you," interrupted Rachel. "Esther refused to give in to a system that said she was a foreigner. She worked her way into the king's palace! There she earned the right to speak to the king about the salvation of her people. She saved the life of her precious cousin Haman from that evil Mordecai. She is the reason we are here today having this conversation and certainly the reason that we celebrate the Feast of Booths every year. What if Esther had bowed to tradition?"

"When I hear you speak, Rachel," Mary responded, "I am grateful that we are asked to keep silent in the synagogue. We would be laughed at for the mistakes and misunderstandings you have carried into this wonderful account of our ancestry."

IN THE CONVERSATION THAT FOLLOWED, HOW WOULD MARY HAVE CORRECTED RACHEL'S STORY?

(Hint: See Esther 2–4; 9.)

How the Wall Was Won

N ehemiah was such a paper trail kind of man," commented Reuben. "Here's a memo he sent back to the king about rebuilding the wall. He kept his bases covered, that's for sure."

Joshua grabbed the parchment out of Reuben's hand. "Let me see that! I've never seen a memo to a king before."

To: The King of Persia
From: Nehemiah, former cupbearer
Regarding: The Jerusalem wall

Thanks again, my king and my friend, for the opportunity to renew my homeland. The journey from your court to this place of destruction was fraught with difficulty, so I'm glad to have arrived safely.

We have finally finished repairing the wall around Jerusalem. The entire task took only fifty-two days from start to finish. It has been difficult, and so have the people, who have been unwilling to work consistently. They have often left their posts and refused to carry weapons.

There have been two men, though, who have furthered the process at every juncture. Sanballet the Horronite and Tobiah the Ammonite have been of more help than I can tell you. They did everything from leading us in prayer to carrying a part of the workload. Someday, my king, I hope you will reward these men.

The dedication ceremony was wonderful as well. Ezra led the procession. There were singers and dancers and Levites. It reminded us of the days of Israel's glory.

We owe that to you, O king. Thank you again.

When Joshua and Reuben finished reading, they looked at each other and exploded in laughter. Reuben spoke first. "What kind of childish prank is this?"

"I don't know," said Joshua, "but let's keep it with us so that our families can have a big laugh, too."

WHAT WAS SO FUNNY ABOUT THE MEMO?

(Hint: See Nehemiah 1–6, 12.)

Will the Real Gomer...

M y name is Gomer," the woman testified at the hearing. She was one of many women who had said the same thing. Each of these women claimed to be the wife of the prophet Hosea. Each wanted to receive the benefits given to a prophet's widow.

A jury of ancients had been gathered to listen to each woman's testimony and determine who, if any, was the real widow.

The woman before them now seemed about the right age. She knew many things about Hosea's life. Because she was less brash and demanding than the others, the ancients seemed to favor her. All that was left was for her to tell her story.

I remember the night my Hosea came to me
with his proposal. I was astounded that a man
of God would want me! I had known so many
men. I had lived such a wretched life. But he
was insistent that his God was calling him to
be my husband.

I became pregnant almost immediately. It
was a boy. I wanted to call him John, but Hosea

named him Jezreel. Jezreel, I thought. Why would you name a child after a town known for a massacre? But Hosea said that was the point. God was promising retribution through naming our firstborn.

My next child was a little girl. I loved the name Abigail, but Hosea said to name her Lo-ammi. I couldn't believe it! He wanted to name her "not loved." What kind of name was that for a beautiful little girl?

As soon as I finished nursing my daughter I became pregnant with a second son. I didn't even pick out a name because I knew Hosea would have something in mind. Sure enough, it was the name Lo-ruhamah meaning "not my people." I shook my head. I lost interest.

I am ashamed to admit it, but you know already—I was not faithful to my husband. There was a hunger inside of me for the love of many men, and so I sought to feed that hunger. I even sold myself into slavery. And do you know what my husband did? He bought me back. He paid the price. He took me home and asked me to live with him faithfully the rest of his life.

I don't know if the Israelite people ever understood God's message to them through my husband. I don't know if they saw that God would love them with a love that pierces the darkest betrayal and brings the wayward home. I saw it. I lived it. I hope they got the message.

The jury listened to her testimony without response, though there were a few raised eyebrows. They then asked the woman to step outside while they deliberated.

WOULD YOU
SAY THIS WAS
THE REAL GOMER?
(Hint: See Hosea 1–2.)

THE SOWER AND THE SEED

LEVEL OF DIFFICULTY: TALENT (HARDEST)

Matthew, James, and John (none of them the disciples of the same name) were walking down the road one day discussing Jesus' parables. They had recounted the wayward son and the vineyard workers. They had pored over the good Samaritan and the pearl of great price. Finally, they had come to the trickiest of all, the sower and the seeds.

They had been walking for two hours and still hadn't put the story together the right way, the way they thought Jesus had told it. They had been trying to remember the ground the seeds fell on, the problem with the seeds, and the meaning of each problem, but they couldn't seem to get all three facts straight.

"Come on, guys, let's take it one category at a time," suggested Matthew. "We know the first seed was the seed along the path."

"Yes," agreed James. "We know that the problem with that seed was that it could grow no roots. The path was beaten down, and the soil was so hard the roots couldn't go down deep."

"Okay," said John. "If that's true, the seeds along the path represent people who turn away from God's Word because the troubles of life knock them around, and they have no root to hold them."

"But wait," corrected Matthew with a very puzzled look. "Wasn't that the problem with the seeds that fell in the thorns?"

James stamped his foot. "No, no, no. This is where we become confused every time, and I'm getting weary. The seeds that fell among the thorns were choked out by the other plants. You have to remember—the *thorns* are the other plants that choked them back."

"So the seeds among the thorns represent the people who have no roots?" asked Matthew.

James sighed patiently. "Matthew, forget the roots for now. Among the thorns they had roots, but they just got choked out. Have we got past the first seed yet?"

"Yes," said John. "We said that the seeds along the path represent people who turn away from God's Word because the troubles of life knock them around, and they have no roots to hold them."

"So what's the second kind of ground?" asked Matthew.

"Whew!" James sighed. He was grateful finally to be moving on. "The second ground was the rocky places. The seeds that fell there represent the people who—"

"—don't understand the Word," interrupted John.

"Are you sure that's right?" asked Matthew. "I was thinking that the seeds among the rocky places were the people who were tempted by wealth and turned back."

James stood with his mouth open, amazed that they were about to get confused *again*. "You two are not making any sense at all. How can this be so difficult?"

"Maybe we should just ask the rabbi when we get to town," suggested Matthew. "He should know."

"But can we at least agree," asked John, "that the good ground represents those of us who hear the Word and understand it?"

James had to laugh. "I have no doubt that we've heard the Word, but I'm not at all sure that, as far as this story goes, we understand it. Let's find the rabbi."

CAN YOU
CLARIFY FOR THE
THREE MEN WHICH
KIND OF GROUND
PRODUCED
WHICH RESULT?
(Hint: See Matthew 13.)

EQUAL PAY

It's not fair!" fumed Elena. "I worked much harder than Phoebe, but we got paid the same."

Elena's father leaned forward, concerned. "Did you get paid what you were promised?"

"Yes, but the point is, I worked *harder* than Phoebe, and I got paid the *same*."

Papa sat back against his chair. "So it's not that Phoebe didn't work hard enough. It's that you didn't get paid enough?"

"Either way, it's the same thing." Elena's pretty face twisted into a pout.

Papa reached out and held her hand in his. He spoke quietly to her rage. "Be careful, Elena. You are angry that someone else got something good that you don't think they deserved."

"So?" she spouted back.

Papa pulled Elena toward his chair until she was standing beside him. "Listen to me, little one. If you are not careful, you will be complaining to God about His own kingdom."

"What does *this* have to do with the kingdom of God, Papa?"

"Jesus told a story once about the kingdom. Let's see if I remember how it goes. A man owned a winepress, and he hired workers for a dollar a day. Some workers came first thing in the morning and started their day's work. Then later in the day, after lunch sometime, the winepress owner hired some more men. Then later, maybe after the afternoon break, he hired more.

"At the end of the day he gathered all the men together to receive their pay. He started with those who had been hired last. He gave them their dollar. He worked himself back to the men who had started that morning. Perhaps they thought that since they had worked longer, they would get more money. But in their hand the foreman only placed the dollar they had been promised."

"See? That's wasn't fair," Elena interjected, shaking her head.

"That's what those men thought," Papa continued. "So they grumbled and complained and wouldn't you know, the owner overheard them. What do you think he said to them, Elena?"

"Did he tell them he was sorry?" she offered.

"No, Ma'am, he didn't. He told them that they had worked for an agreed amount, and he wasn't changing it. He told them that it was his money, and if wanted to pay the latecomers a whole dollar he could. He asked them if they resented his generosity. What do you think of that?"

"So what you're saying is," Elena paused to think, "it's not that I was treated badly. Instead, it's that Phoebe was treated better than she may have deserved. And you're saying that God gets to make that choice."

"Yes," answered Papa. "Be careful snubbing the grace others receive. At one time or another, all of us receive something good we don't deserve. Be glad when you do. Be glad when your friend does."

WHAT
CORRECTIONS
WOULD YOU MAKE
TO PAPA'S
VERSION OF
THE STORY?
(Hint: See Matthew 20.)

BEST SEATS
IN THE HOUSE

Elizabeth was famous for twisting someone's words when it suited her needs. She once told a friend that the Golden Rule was "Do unto others, and you can expect them to do the same unto you." In her village her reputation for bending life's truths was legendary.

But she had another claim to fame as well. Elizabeth was even better known for the inappropriate times at which she spouted her customized wisdom. She had brought more conversations to an embarrassed stop than anyone else in Bel-hiam. Because of this, most of the village went to any community event filled with anticipation of Elizabeth's potential faux pas.

So it was with the wedding of Paul of Bethany and Susannah of Bel-hiam. When the day arrived, everyone showed up in his or her finest regalia. The wine was the best ever tasted. The food was the most delectable that could be found. In the midst of it all stood Elizabeth, keeping a running commentary on the guests, the servants, and the families involved.

No matter the conversation, though, she had one eye toward the banquet table. It was being piled high with fruit and vegetables, hummus, and lamb. Elizabeth repeatedly asked what time they were serving, and whenever she got the answer, "Soon," she began to sidle her way closer to the doorway of the banquet room.

She was standing just beside the entrance when she heard a familiar voice behind her. "Elizabeth, what are you doing?" It was the rabbi from her synagogue.

Elizabeth smiled at him with one eye toward the feast. "Oh, Rabbi, I'm watching the preparations. Doesn't everything look wonderful?"

"You aren't positioning yourself to grab the best seat in the house, are you, Elizabeth?"

"Now, Rabbi," she responded, "didn't Jesus give us specific instructions about taking seats at a wedding feast?"

"Yes, He did, Elizabeth. I'm just not sure what you think those instructions were."

"Everybody knows that. He said that when someone invites you to a wedding, to accept the place of honor graciously. If you don't, then you will be left with the last seat, and you won't hear a thing that's going on.

"I've always agreed with Jesus about that," Elizabeth continued. "It's the good guest who wants to be truly involved in every aspect of the celebration." She finished talking as the head servant walked toward the doorway to call the guests.

"Elizabeth, come with me," said the rabbi. "Let's go see what the Scriptures actually say about taking your seat at a wedding feast."

The rabbi and a very unwilling Elizabeth walked toward the back of the house just as the guests entered the feast.

WHAT DID JESUS ACTUALLY SAY ABOUT THE SEATS AT A WEDDING FEAST?

(Hint: See Luke 14.)

THE FIRST CHRISTIAN MARTYR

LEVEL OF DIFFICULTY: TALENT (HARDEST)

What's a martyr?" asked Stephanie.

"A martyr is someone who dies for what he or she believes," answered Aunt Nola.

"Why would anyone be killed for believing in something?" Stephanie questioned.

"Beliefs are powerful things, Stephanie. Jesus was killed because He believed He was God in the flesh."

"But Jesus *was* God in the flesh," countered Stephanie again.

"Yes, we know that He was, but the people who killed Him didn't know or believe that was true. In fact, they considered what Jesus preached to be dangerous and even blasphemous. Don't ever underestimate the power of faith."

"So a martyr is someone who tells their beliefs even though they will be killed for them?" reasoned Stephanie.

Nola nodded. "That's right. You are named after the first martyr. His name was Stephen. He stood tall for his faith, and he was killed for it."

Stephanie was enthralled. "Tell me how it happened! Please?"

Nola hesitated. "It's not a pretty topic, you know. I haven't even thought about it in a long time. It was such a sad ending for such a good man."

Stephanie said nothing in the hopes that Nola would continue.

She did. "Stephen was a holy and good man. He worked miracles and had a great faith. He was wiser than the religious leaders who stood against him. As people will do, when they couldn't win an argument fairly, they began to lie. They talked people into telling lies about Stephen. They made it sound like Stephen was denying his Jewish heritage and disparaging our forefathers. In all of their accusations Stephen remained silent. He did not speak a word until they dragged him outside of the city to stone him. As they threw their stones he cried out as Jesus did from the cross, 'Lord, why have You forsaken me?' "

Stephanie was predictably horrified. "Did anyone try to stop them?"

Nola took Stephanie's hand in hers. "Paul of Tarsus was there. I'm sure he tried to stop them, but an angry mob is difficult to control. Stephen died that day and all because he believed that Jesus was God's Son, our Messiah. Many more have died since for believing the same thing."

CAN YOU
CORRECT A FEW
DETAILS OF
NOLA'S ACCOUNT?
(Hint: See Acts 6–7.)

A SISTER IN CHRIST

LEVEL OF DIFFICULTY: TALENT (HARDEST)

"A letter! A letter!" Abigail shouted, running toward the vineyard. "We got a letter from Lydia!"

All the workers, mostly extended family members, gathered around. "Wonderful!" said Silas on behalf of them all. "What does it say?"

Abigail looked at both of her hands as if they were someone else's. "Oh no. I left it on the table. I was in such a rush to come and tell you that I left the letter behind!"

The disappointment among the family was palpable.

"It's so far back to the house, Abigail," Silas reasoned. "Could you remember what the letter says, and then we can read it for ourselves when we come home later?"

"Well, let's see. . . ," Abigail said, thinking out loud. "The big news is that she was baptized!"

Everyone cheered.

"It was near her home in Pisidia," Abigail continued looking up into the sky as if the letter were written somewhere in the clouds. "I believe she was baptized in the Jordan River just like Jesus. It must have been wonderful!"

This time the crowd looked confused.

"Who baptized her?" asked Silas.

"Two apostles, James and John, had come to her town.

They met with her Bible study group and then baptized her and her family."

Silas was looking more and more doubtful. "Anything else?"

"Only that the apostles are living with her now and leading the church in Pisidia."

The workers started back to their tasks. Silas smiled at his excited wife. "Abigail, you run on home now, and we'll read that letter together when we get home. I think in your excitement you may have missed a few of the finer points."

CAN YOU
FIND THE POINTS
THAT ABIGAIL
MISSED?
(Hint: See Acts 16.)

WHO WAS APOLLOS?

The historians gathered in the upstairs room were almost as dusty as the unused parchments on the shelves. These were the men who reveled in the details of past lives and ancient events. They could talk for hours about the jots and the tittles of not only the laws of their people but also the historical context of each one of those laws.

And now a greater challenge lay before them. They had been gathered to research the present growth in the church and its strongest influences. They were out of their element, really. Writing about the past with its documentation and archaeological evidence was one thing. Studying the church would include sorting through research, interviews, and word-of-mouth, secondhand histories. None of the musty old men in that upstairs room wanted to dirty their hands with facts so controvertible.

"Let's jump right in and try one," said Alexander, with a tone of desperation. "Who is the first on the list?"

A quiet voice in the corner answered, "Apollos."

Audible groans passed around the room. There were so many stories circulating about Apollos that most felt it would be impossible to separate fact from fiction.

"Who's going first?" Alexander asked in a weary voice.

"I'll go," offered Timothy. As the youngest member of the group, at age sixty-two, he was the least jaded and the least tired. "I've learned a lot about Apollos in the last three days. First of all, he is from Alexandria. He is basically uneducated, except that he followed John the Baptist for about three years. He is gifted musically and often accompanies his sermons with psalms and hymns. Ananias and Sapphira of Jerusalem fame mentored him in his faith. He is almost as influential as Paul the apostle, so much so that some churches have prided themselves on being baptized by Apollos rather than Paul." Timothy sat back in his chair.

"What?" Hester blurted out. "Where did you get all that information?"

Timothy was unaffected by his colleague's outburst. "From interviews and manuscripts and correspondence, just like I'm sure you did, Hester. Please fill us in on your research."

Hester shook her head in disbelief. "According to my sources, Apollos is a native of Ephesus, but he taught in Alexandria. He was voted in as one of the twelve apostles after Judas's death. Most of his training came from the time he spent at a Jewish synagogue under the tutelage of Barnabas. He is vehemently against baptizing anyone himself for the specific purpose of reducing conflict among the brethren."

Hester and Timothy scowled at each other across the table. Alexander wilted visibly. "Anyone else?" he asked.

Basgar cleared his throat and then began to speak in

an irritatingly shrill voice made worse by the rising tension in the room. "I have done some extensive research into Apollos's background. According to the records I have accessed, Apollos was actually an early disciple of Paul, the apostle. He grew up in Rome where his father was an unorthodox Greek, but his mother, Lois, was a Christian." Basgar looked at no one as he completed his report.

Alexander looked around the table and asked, "Does anyone know one fact about Apollos that is certain?"

DID THEY
KNOW ANY
ACCURATE
FACTS ABOUT
APOLLOS?
(Hint: See Acts 18.)

HERO OR GOAT?

LEVEL OF DIFFICULTY: TALENT (HARDEST)

The judge looked sternly at the defendant. "Baruch Barabbas, you are charged with illegal seizure and stoning. How do you plead?"

"Not guilty, your Honor," answered Baruch.

"What do you have to say for yourself?" asked the judge.

"In the first place, Judge, I wasn't part of the group that stoned Paul and left him for dead. You can ask my wife. I was at home in front of the fire."

"Were you in town to see the events that transpired before the stoning?" questioned the judge sternly.

"Yes, I will admit, your Honor, that I was there earlier on, but that doesn't make me guilty of seizure and stoning."

"If you were not at the site when Paul was stoned, Baruch, then you are correct in your plea. But it would help this court to know about the events that transpired that day. Please fill us in as best you can."

"Well, Judge," he began, clearing his throat, "Paul was speaking in Lystra, and his colleague, Barsabas, was standing nearby. Paul told a man who had been deaf all his life to answer his questions. The man did it! I was amazed myself. That man had *never* been able to hear, but he answered Paul every time. Some of the people there were more than amazed. They became convinced that Paul and the other man were gods. They called Paul, Hermes, and they called Barsabas, Hercules.

"The priests from the temple of Zeus began bringing sacrifices to the men. Once the preachers realized the misunderstanding, they used the attention to preach even more and louder. I guess they thought they'd use the situation to their best advantage. I can't say that I blame them. They believed in their message, and they wanted as many people to listen as possible. The crowd got worked into a bit of a frenzy, I guess.

"Then some men showed up from Ephesus and Philippi. You know how a crowd is, Judge. Once they are in a frenzy, they can be turned so quickly. Well, these newcomers turned that same crowd against Paul and his friend. The same people that were bringing him sacrifices one minute were dragging Paul outside of the city and leaving him for dead.

"I really don't understand it myself, your Honor. How could they leave a man all crumpled up outside the city after they were calling him a god that afternoon?"

The judge eyed Baruch suspiciously. "You seem to know an awful lot about how and where Paul was left after the stoning for a man who was at home in front of a fire."

HOW TRUTHFUL WAS BARUCH'S TESTIMONY?

(Hint: See Acts 14.)

Shipwreck on Malta

LEVEL OF DIFFICULTY: TALENT (HARDEST)

I t's a map!" shouted Ahmed.

"It's a diary!" corrected Iman.

"I think it's both," Ahmed acquiesced. "No matter how you look at this parchment, it's a part of the journey of Paul the Apostle. It must be the map he followed, and the notes must be the diary of what happened at each port. It's really hard to read, though."

"Let's go tell someone!" encouraged Iman with excitement.

Ahmed held the map out of Iman's reach. "Wait. Give me a chance to look before you go dragging it off to some rabbi or something." Ahmed began scribbling on another parchment. "Let's copy down the notes and the basic map and *then* take it to someone. That way I can do my own research."

Ahmed and Iman spent the next hour deciphering the scribbled notes and arguing over their interpretation. When they had copied the notes, they read over their copy of the diary/map with satisfaction.

Sidon: I visited with friends. It was a great time.
Myra: We transferred to a Viking ship sailing for Italy.

Fair Haven: I warned the guards that we were in for a difficult and dangerous journey, but no one would listen. We set sail tomorrow, and I believe it spells disaster.

Cauda: A storm caught us in its force. We were driven along by it. We began to throw cargo overboard and lashed the boat together with ropes just in case we hit one of the sandbars at Syrtis. We fought the storm and drifted for three days. The men began to lose hope. I prophesied to them this morning that not one life would be lost. I told them that an angel appeared to me during the night to tell me that I would stand trial before Caesar and that none of them would be lost at sea. They wouldn't believe me again.

Malta: Finally we spotted land. Before we could get to the shore, though, the ship ran aground. We all swam for shore. It was rainy and cold, but the islanders were kind and built a fire for us. As I was throwing wood on the fire, a snake lodged its fangs into my hand. The islanders interpreted this to mean that God was punishing me for murder. After I shook the snake into the fire with no ill effects, they decided that I must be a god. After that, we were taken to the home of Publius, the chief official. He entertained us for three days. While I was there I prayed for his father who was suffering from leprosy. When his father was healed all the rest of the sick on the island were cured as well. After twelve months there, we set sail with all the supplies we needed. The ship we used was

another Viking ship with a figurehead of the gods
Castor and Pollux.

Syracuse: We stayed three days and set sail for
Rhegium.

Puteoli: We met some brothers who kidnapped us and
took us to Rome. I was fearful but arrived safely.

Rome: I'm in a house by myself, which is a blessing, but
am guarded both day and night. The trial will
begin soon.

IF THIS
WERE AN
ACTUAL DIARY
OF PAUL'S, HOW
ACCURATELY DID
AHMED AND IMAN
TRANSCRIBE IT?
(Hint: See Acts 27–28.)

UP ON THE ROOF

LEVEL OF DIFFICULTY: TALENT (HARDEST)

Cyrus rushed around the room gathering his sandals and tunic. "The tour will be here in just a few minutes, Benjamin, but I have to go. Could you cover for me?"

Benjamin looked horrified. "Cover for you? This is only the second time I have been in this house. How am I going to lead a tour? You cannot go. You have to wait until the tour is over!"

Cyrus stopped rushing and put his hands on the shoulders of his young friend. "I *must* go, Benjamin. I have no choice. Now, it hasn't even been that long ago since these events took place. On the tour will be people from a neighboring village. Just remember to show them the roof and talk about the dream. You've heard the story many times. I know you can handle it."

In less than a minute, Cyrus was out the door and Benjamin was standing alone. Soon he heard excited voices and knew that his travelers were arriving.

"Welcome!" Benjamin said with his best smile. He dared not take a hand for fear they would feel him shaking. And so, without further ado, he began his spiel. "This is the home of Simeon the tanner. On more than one occasion, Simeon hosted Simon Peter, one of Jesus' closest disciples, here in this very house and in this very room. Please make yourself at home."

Before the people could be seated, Ben asked, "Would you like to see the roof?" He saw excited nods all around. The group followed him as he wound through the house looking for the stairs to the roof. Finally the group was all gathered at the legendary site.

"So this is the actual place where it happened?" one woman asked Benjamin.

"Uh, yes, this is it," he answered, wracking his brain for the details. "You might remember that Peter rose early one morning and came up on this very roof. It was here that God spoke to him in a dream."

"What did God say. . .exactly?" the same woman asked.

"Well, it wasn't so much what God said as it was what God showed Peter. He showed him a magic carpet with a large pig riding on it. Four times Peter saw this carpet and this pig. Then God told Peter to kill and eat the pig."

The crowd of mostly Jewish tourists gasped.

"Yes, indeed, He did." Benjamin continued, encouraged by their response. "And Peter told God he had never eaten anything unclean. That's when God spoke the message that changed Peter's ministry. God said, 'Do not call anything impure that I have made clean.'

"Just then, as Peter was pondering the dream, two men from Cornelius's household arrived and asked Peter to come with them. Understand that Cornelius was a Gentile, so Peter also thought him to be unclean. When

Peter arrived at Cornelius's house in Joppa, a large group of people was waiting to hear him teach. Cornelius told Peter that God had given him instructions to invite him to come. God had even told Cornelius where to find Peter.

"Once Peter was there, he understood what his dream meant. God was telling him not to show favoritism toward food or people but to know that God made everything clean.

"Feel free to visit up here on the roof as long as you like. I'll be downstairs when you are ready to move on."

Benjamin rushed down the stairs and let out a huge sigh of relief. He hoped he had told the story correctly.

HAD HE?
(Hint: See Acts 10.)

HIGH PROFILE PRISONER MISSING

LEVEL OF DIFFICULTY: TALENT (HARDEST)

To say that Rhoda was a little flighty would be an understatement. She could get caught up in the moment and forget everything that came before or the consequences that would come afterward. That's how she was the night Peter came to the house where she was a servant.

According to all accounts pieced together, Pontius Pilate had thrown Peter and James into prison. Peter was in one cell and James was in another. The night before his trial Peter was not only bound with two chains, but he was also sleeping between two guards. Sometime during the night someone struck Peter in the side. When he looked up he saw an angel. The room was filled with light, and the chains fell off Peter's wrists. The angel told him to put on his clothes, his shoes, and his coat and to follow along.

Peter and the angel walked right out of the prison, passing guards all along the way. They came to the gate of the city, which was made of iron, and it mysteriously opened to let them go through. They flew above the city until the angel left Peter at the door of a house. It wasn't until then that Peter realized it wasn't a dream at all: He really was out of jail!

The angel had deposited Peter at Mary's house (she was John Mark's mother). In that very house Christians were praying for Peter. Peter knocked at the entrance and, wouldn't you know, Rhoda was the one who came to the door. Before she opened it Peter told her who he was. She got so excited that she ran back to tell the others—before she even let Peter into the house! Can you imagine? The man gets miraculously released from prison, makes his way to a safe place, and the servant *forgets* to let him in! Poor Peter had to continue knocking until the rest of the group came to the front of the house and finally greeted him. He told them the story of his release and then left.

The next morning the jail was frenzied. Pilate looked everywhere for Peter. When they couldn't find him, he ordered the guards executed.

What a story! And what about that Rhoda?

WHAT PARTS
OF THIS STORY
ARE INACCURATE?
(Hint: See Acts 12.)

SOLUTIONS

ON THE FIRST DAY. . . : Rabbi Ithamar incorrectly referred to the fall of Adam and Eden instead of Adam and Eve. He also confused the first six days of creation. Here is the correct order: God created. . .

> Day 1: light and darkness;
> Day 2: separation between earth and sky;
> Day 3: land, seas, and plants;
> Day 4: sun, moon, and stars;
> Day 5: fish and birds;
> Day 6: people and animals.

Also, there is no record of God causing a great celebration on the seventh day. The Bible says that is when God rested.

LOST INNOCENCE: The forbidden tree was in the center of the garden, not on the eastern border. The serpent said that Eve could be like God and know good from evil but not see into the future. The Bible says Adam's and Eve's eyes were opened in awareness, not that they opened their eyes for the first time. They used fig rather than palm leaves for their first suit of clothes.

BROTHERLY LOVE: Cain was older than Abel. It was Abel whom the Lord favored for offering fat portions of meat. The Lord did not regard Cain for his offerings of fruit. Cain became angry and killed his brother. The Lord told Cain that the earth would not yield its strength to him, and so Cain went from the Lord's sight into the land of Nod.

UP IN SMOKE: Lot was actually the nephew of Abraham and the son of Haran, Abraham's brother. The cities of Sodom and Gomorrah were incredibly evil rather than righteous, but their destruction had nothing to do with Lot. The cities were not destroyed at night but in the hours after dawn, after Lot and his family had left Sodom.

TRADE RIGHTS: Esau's twin brother was Jacob, not Isaac. Isaac was their father, and he was indeed the son of Abraham. Jacob had made a stew, not a steak, but Esau did trade his birthright for the meal anyway.

REMEMBERING JOSEPH: Potiphar actually bought Joseph as a slave; he did not hire him as an employee. When Potiphar's wife threw herself at Joseph, he left behind his coat, not his shoes. In jail he was in a cell with the king's cupbearer and baker, and not the butcher. When those two men had their dreams, Joseph predicted what would happen but didn't make the events come true. Only the cupbearer was reinstated to his position in the palace. The baker was killed. Joseph made his way into the palace by interpreting a dream of the king. When Joseph interpreted the dream, which explained the famine, the king gave him a position over food conservation rather than assign him as cupbearer.

ROLLIN' DOWN THE RIVER: Both of Moses's parents were of the house of Levi. They were Hebrews, not Edomites. Moses's mother hid him for three months, not six. Moses fled to Midian, not Kadesh-Barnea, where he met Reuel. Finally, God came in the form of a burning bush, not a thunderstorm.

FIGHTING LIKE BROTHERS: The brothers were Aaron and Moses. The stick gave it away because Aaron's rod miraculously budded and produced almonds. The brothers tricked Pharaoh into letting the Hebrews go. They tried to get their people to the Promised Land. They were cross when Aaron stood with his sister Miriam against Moses. They walked away from Egypt with all of the Hebrew people.

PARTING THE RED SEA: Pharaoh was the king of Egypt. He was the one who wanted to chase after the Israelites after he originally told them that they could leave. There is no record of an Abar or a Sihon. Neither is there a record of divisions among the Israelites at this point. There is no record of God's voice coming from the sky, nor is there mention of thunder and lightning when Moses raised his staff.

Bible Detective

IN THE PRESENCE OF JEHOVAH: Moses was on the mountain forty days rather than thirty. While Moses was on the mountain, he had no food or water. God didn't prepare a banquet. But it is true that Moses's face glowed from God's glory and that he had to wear a veil.

GOD TALKS TO A LITTLE BOY. . .BUT HOW?: Samuel was sleeping at the tabernacle but not at the foot of Eli's mat. It is true that God called three times and Eli helped Samuel know it was God's voice. Samuel responded, "Speak, Lord. I am listening." God's message was of judgment on Eli's family. When Eli heard that, he accepted the fate of his family with resignation.

THE GIANT: David was the son of Jesse rather than Jeremiah. He actually had three older brothers go off to war, not one. The giant's name was Goliath, and he fought on the side of the Philistines, not for Israel. His whole body, not just his head, was measured as six cubits and a span. Goliath was a Philistine; David was an Israelite. Instead of arrows, David used a slingshot and five smooth stones. Also, David convinced Saul of his strength by explaining how God protected him as he killed both a lion and a bear, not men twice his size.

A SUFFERING SAINT: This is no letter from Job due to the many skewed facts. To begin, Job had seven sons and three daughters rather than the other way around. These children were killed by a windstorm, not an enemy attack. He didn't doubt himself during his suffering but kept insisting that he had done nothing wrong. Also, he wasn't left in poverty. All of his children and riches were restored. But the big giveaway is that Job's three friends were not a comfort to him. In fact, they increased his suffering by telling him he must have done something wrong when he hadn't. They fought with him, targeting him with self-doubt rather than reassuring him. Whoever wrote this letter did not write it from Job's perspective.

IN THE LIONS' DEN: The story of Daniel in the lions' den happened in Babylon, and not in Egypt, so there was a king on the throne and

208

not a pharaoh. The ruling was that the king be prayed to for thirty days rather than a year. Daniel faced Jerusalem and prayed three times a day rather than ten. A stone was put over the mouth of the cave rather than a fire. We have no record that Daniel was cradled in a lion's paws, only that God closed the mouths of the animals. While the king was elated that Daniel was alive and well, he didn't name Daniel as his successor. Finally, the satraps and their families were thrown into the den, but they were crushed by the lions before they hit the ground, and not eaten.

GIFTS OF THE MAGI: The Magi actually saw Jesus at a house rather than a stable. We know the Magi were warned about Herod in a dream, but we are not told that an angel was involved. It was an angel rather than the Magi, though, who warned Joseph to take Jesus away. Joseph took Jesus to Egypt at that time and not to Nazareth. Finally, Herod ordered all baby boys up to two years old, rather than six months, to be put to death.

BAPTISM OF A KING: The Bible does not tell us that Jesus came to John walking across the water. We also do not know whether Jesus bowed low or asked to be baptized. John's response to Jesus was one of hesitation. He didn't feel worthy to baptize Jesus. God did perform a miracle after the baptism but not the one the old man described. Instead, the heavens opened, and the Spirit of God descended like a dove, proclaiming how pleased God was with Jesus.

THE OBEDIENT STORM: Only the opening scene is skewed. Jesus was below deck sleeping, and the disciples were up above battling the storm. The rest of the story is correct.

MUSTARD-SEED FAITH: At one time Jesus said that with faith as a mustard seed a believer could tell a mountain to move, and it would. At another time He said that with faith as a mustard seed a believer could tell a mulberry tree to plant itself in the sea and it would.

Bible Detective

HOW YOU GONNA KEEP 'EM DOWN ON THE FARM?: Ana had a few of the details wrong. In Jesus' parable of the prodigal son, it was the younger son who left home and spent his wealth excessively. The son did not give away his money, as in donations, but rather he wasted his wealth on wild living. He also worked with pigs, not cows.

SISTERS: Mary and Martha did have a disagreement, but Scripture does not record it as being as intense as the townswomen described. Martha was, indeed, preparing dinner—but there is no record of what she served. She did involve Jesus in that she asked Him to have Mary help her, but He simply told Martha to leave Mary alone. He said that she had chosen to do the best thing by listening to Him. There is no record that He separated them or that they severed their relationship in light of the disagreement.

RESURRECTION IN BETHANY: The Bible doesn't say that Jesus was unable to come immediately—He consciously delayed His visit. Lazarus had been buried four days rather than a week. Mary, as well as Martha, did go out and meet Jesus and talk with Him. When Jesus called Lazarus out, He said something closer to "Lazarus, come forth" than "Your time has come." When Lazarus came out of the tomb, he was still wrapped in graveclothes. The meeting of the religious leaders was actually to discuss how to get rid of Jesus and the political and religious waves He was causing rather than how to honor Him.

TO BE BORN AGAIN: Mary heard some of the conversation but in the totally wrong context. There is no hint in Scripture that Nicodemus was not a godly man. Nicodemus went to Jesus to discuss Jesus' relationship with God. Jesus took the opportunity to tell him about the necessity of being born again and how God had provided for this rebirth through His love. He told Nicodemus that God gave His only Son out of love. Mary missed the point entirely.

WHEN THE ROOSTER CROWED: Both of the first two inquiries to Peter were made by females. The second and third times (there were only

210

three inquiries) occurred when Peter was out at the gate. We are not told that Peter entered the place where Jesus' trial was taking place. It was when the rooster crowed, rather than when the sun rose, that Peter realized he had fulfilled Jesus' prophecy about him.

THE PRICE OF THE CHRIST: According to the Scriptures, Judas Iscariot approached the chief priests, not the other way around. Thirty pieces of silver was the agreed upon price, but there is no record of Judas trying to back out before the betrayal.

ONE PRISONER GOES FREE: Barabbas was in jail for insurrection and murder rather than kidnapping and thievery. It was Pontius Pilate, and not Caesar, who was running the trial. We have no record that Barabbas spoke in Jesus' defense.

FRIEND AND FOLLOWER: Jesus actually cast seven demons out of Mary rather than fifteen. She did attend Jesus' crucifixion, but we have no record that she ran screaming from the scene. She did see Jesus after His Resurrection, but she mistook Him for a gardener and not a guard.

A HUSBAND'S LIE AND A KING'S MISTAKE: Abraham said Sarah was his sister and not his cousin. God didn't tell the king to wash in the Jordan River but, instead, to go to Abraham and have him pray for the king. The king neither ran Abraham out nor gave him nothing. He made peace with Abraham and gave him gifts and money instead.

NO LOOKING BACK: The hermit was less than honest about most of the story. Rather than God Himself, it was an angel who told Lot to flee and not onto the plain but into the mountains—though Lot begged to stop in a small town, Zoar, on the plain first. It was the angel who warned them about turning around. Lot's wife looked back at Sodom and Gomorrah, and became a pillar of salt, well before God brought destruction on the cities. Lot was traveling with his wife and two daughters. There was no little boy. There is no explosion mentioned in Genesis. Instead, a rain of burning sulfur ("fire and brimstone") destroyed the cities.

THE WIFE HUNT: We really don't know the name of the man named Elihu in the story. We only know that he was Abraham's chief servant. He was told specifically to go back to Abraham's homeland rather than avoid it. And he took camels rather than horses to the well. The sign he asked for had nothing to do with how the girl carried the water. The sign was that when he asked for water, she would offer to get water for his camels, too. Finally, the new bride's name was Rebekah and not Rachel.

I'M DAD'S FAVORITE: The Lord told Rebekah that the older son would serve the younger. Esau was the older son and not Jacob. They are switched in the story. While Isaac instructed Esau to go out and fetch game for him to bless him, Jacob brought savory food in to Isaac under the mask of Esau and stole the blessing. Jacob did not bring a fine blanket made of linen. He used the skins of kids instead of feathers to make his skin appear hairy.

DREAM A LITTLE DREAM . . . : Joseph was a son of Jacob or Israel rather than Edom. Joseph's brothers never intended to sell him to the Romans. Instead, they threw him into a cistern and then sold him as a slave to members of a traveling caravan. Eventually, he was sold to Potiphar, an officer of Pharaoh and captain of the guard. Joseph was sent to prison because of accusations of sexual misconduct rather than thievery. The letter was also incorrect concerning Joseph's dreams. Joseph dreamed that he and his brothers were out in the field, and his brothers' sheaves bowed down to his. In his second dream, he saw the sun, moon, and eleven stars bow down to him. Finally, the letter stated that Joseph told the butler that he would be promoted, when in actuality Joseph told the prisoner that within three days Pharaoh would restore him to his original position.

TWO BRAVE MIDWIVES: The Bible tells us that Shiphrah and Puah did *not* obey the command. When the king confronted them, they told him that the Hebrew women gave birth so quickly that the babies were born before the midwives arrived. Amazingly, he did not punish the midwives, and God blessed them for their obedience to Him.

GOD IN A BUSH?: The bush was not burning up slowly. It wasn't burning up at all. It was just on fire. The voice calling Moses came directly out of the bush. The voice told Moses to take off his sandals rather than his coat and tunic. It also told him to stay away rather than come closer. When God identified Himself to Moses, Moses hid his face rather than running away. Finally, Moses was frightened and resistant rather than exhilarated at God's request.

THE PLAGUES: The old men stopped arguing because they agreed on a fact that is incorrect: Snakes were not one of the plagues. This was the only fact, though, on which Zechariah was incorrect. There were ten plagues, beginning with the water being turned into blood, and followed by frogs, lice, flies, diseased livestock, boils, hail, locusts, darkness, and the death of the firstborn. Lastly, the waters were turned into blood, not wine, and it was Aaron who struck the waters with his rod, not Moses.

THE GREAT ESCAPE, AND OTHER MIRACLES: In the list of plagues, flies should come after lice rather than after locusts. The snakes didn't eat each other. Instead, Aaron's serpent/rod ate all the others. Pharaoh's army did not survive the rushing back of the waters. They were all killed in the midst of the sea.

IS THIS THE ARK OF THE COVENANT?: Whatever Jonas found was, first of all, too small to be the Ark of the Covenant. The ark was about four feet long and two feet wide. It was made of wood but covered with pure gold instead of bronze. There were two rings on each side, rather than one on each end, so that the priests could put poles through the rings and carry the ark without touching it. While Jonas was hoping to see inside the ark, he would never have found Elijah's mantle. The ark at one time had the Ten Commandments, though, as well as some manna and Aaron's rod.

SHOUTING DOWN THE WALLS: It was Joshua, and not Jeremiah, who led the Hebrews around the city of Jericho. The Hebrews carried the Ark of the Covenant rather than the altar from the temple. On the seventh day the people walked around the city seven times instead of eight. Finally, the priests blew trumpets rather than beat on drums.

RUTH AND BOAZ: Ruth was married to Naomi's son rather than her nephew. Ruth did work diligently, but not shearing sheep. Instead, Boaz (who was from the clan of Elimelech, not Elijah) noted how hard she worked gathering grain. Ruth herself uncovered Boaz's feet, and slept by his feet on the threshing floor. She did not engage him in conversation in order to present a good appearance. Boaz met with the ten elders of the town, but not to get their approval. Such a meeting was customary to work out an agreement with another man of the area who was closer in relation to Naomi's late husband Elimelech than Boaz was. When that relative declined to marry Ruth, Boaz was free to follow his heart and do so.

THE FIRST KING OF ISRAEL: Josie was right about one thing. Saul really did hide in the baggage and had to be brought out to be recognized by the people as king. But Jael was correct about the rest. Saul did go hunting for lost donkeys. He did talk to Samuel in order to find them. The three signs Samuel told Saul to watch for were just as Jael listed them.

SOLOMON'S TEMPLE: King David prepared the plans for the temple, but he did not begin construction. King Solomon had the temple built. The wood used for paneling was cedar, not pine. Much of that was overlaid with gold, not silver. The Most Holy Place held two statues of cherubim, but none of palm trees. It did not hold a carving of Moses. Since the priests did enter the Holy of Holies at least once a year, they would know if the Ark of the Covenant resided there, even if Caleb and his "tourists" never would.

JEZEBEL REMEMBERED: Jezebel's crown was not listed among her remains. Jezebel was the wife of Ahab, and not his daughter. She was neither responsible for the death of Elijah nor did she offer his remains in idol worship.

PASSING THE MANTLE: Elijah anointed Elisha to be a prophet, not a king. Elisha was plowing with twelve yoke of oxen rather than six. Elisha cooked and served his oxen, rather than taming them as pets.

SWEPT OFF HIS FEET: Elisha was with Elijah the whole time, so Elijah wasn't alone. The body of water involved was the Jordan River rather than the Dead Sea. Elijah hit the water with his cloak, and the sea separated. He didn't walk across the water. He was carried to heaven in a whirlwind and chariot of fire, not by a golden horseman. And only Elijah's cloak was left, not his shoes.

THE THREE AMIGOS: The statue that King Nebuchadnezzar built was made of gold, not silver. The people were required to worship it when they heard the loud music of horns, flutes, harps, lyres, pipes, and "all kinds of music." Shadrach, Meshach, and Abednego were not thrown into the ocean but into a burning fiery furnace where God protected them. Also, the king saw four figures rather than five: the three men and the figure of the Son of God. There was no angel with the men. Finally, upon seeing this great act of faith, Nebuchadnezzar believed. He did not question the men or think that they were evil. The king ultimately promoted the three young men, but in the province of Babylon, not Ammon.

MAKING SACRIFICES: Malachi condemned his people for bringing less than their best to God. He mentioned bringing spotted or diseased animals, citing this as a sign of contempt. Jacob should have known better.

A Trusting Husband: Joseph was a righteous man, the Bible tells us. An angel did come to Joseph, but he told him to name the child Jesus. A donkey did speak to a prophet named Balaam in the Old Testament, but not to Joseph. It was Mary, not Joseph, who visited her relative, Elizabeth, and received confirmation that Jesus was the Messiah. The angel did not tell Joseph to raise Jesus as a carpenter or to love him as his own, though most people believe he did those things.

He Could Not Be Tempted: Jesus fasted for forty days and nights, not seventy. Satan tempted Jesus to turn stones, not dirt, into bread, not stew. Satan also tempted Him to worship him in exchange for all the glories of the earth, but there is no record that he asked Jesus to serve as his prophet. Angels did come to attend Jesus after Satan departed, but there is no record that they guided Him home.

Fish for Five Thousand: The Scriptures teach that Jesus knew exactly what He was going to do. He only asked the disciples for help to test them. Philip actually told Jesus that feeding the crowd would take eight months' wages rather than merely one month's pay. It was Andrew who brought the child with the lunch. The lunch consisted of five loaves of bread and two fish, and not three fish. The crowd was told to take as much as they wanted from the beginning. There were twelve baskets of leftovers gathered so that nothing would be wasted.

A Missionary by the Well: The well was near Sychar in Samaria, not Jericho. There is no record that the woman asked Jesus to pay for the water, and there is no record that Jesus healed the woman of any diseases. Jesus told the woman that she had had five husbands rather than three, and that she was living with one man rather than two. Jesus stayed in the town for two days, rather than a week.

For a Pound of Perfume: It was Mary, and not Enid, who anointed Jesus' feet. Lazarus only had two sisters that we know of, Martha and Mary. There is no mention in the Bible that Martha was embarrassed by the anointing. Judas questioned the use of perfume not because the money to purchase it could have been used for missions, but because those same coins could have been given to the poor. In Judas's mind, though, he wanted to keep the money for himself. He was in charge of the funds and often liked to keep some money for himself.

FIRST, A PERSECUTOR: There is no record that Saul was present at Jesus' crucifixion, but he was present at Stephen's stoning. He didn't throw the moneychangers out of the temple. Jesus was the one who did that. Also, he did carry letters to Damascus but they weren't from Herod. These letters, which were from the high priest, didn't have to do with burning churches to the ground. At that time the Christian churches met in people's homes. Finally, when Saul carried away religious prisoners, he usually carried them to Jerusalem rather than to Rome.

A BLIND CONVERSION: Saul was stopped by a light from heaven rather than fire from the ground. The voice that spoke to him, that of Jesus, said neither "Arise and worship" nor "I am that I am." The men traveling with Paul heard what was happening, though they saw no one. Even though Saul had been struck blind, he traveled on to Damascus. There he was ministered to by a man named Ananias rather than a woman named Anna. His blindness was healed after three days rather than two months. Finally, Paul never became a high priest.

SAFE HAVEN: While Silas did come to Antioch later, Paul and Barnabas did the first work there. Paul got help from the church in Jerusalem rather than the church in Bethlehem. Also, Vanessa had it backward. It was the Jews who wanted the Greeks to live by Jewish law in order to be saved.

THE ALMOST JAILBREAK: The prison was in Philippi rather than Rome, and the prisoners were Paul and Silas, instead of Paul and Barnabas. Paul had actually cast a demon out of a girl, and that is what incited the riot that led to their arrest. Lastly, the jailer was going to kill himself with a sword rather than a spear.

FROM THE MOUTHS OF BABEL: The people set out to build a city and one tower, not three towers. Because they were in the desert and had no stones, they made bricks instead from the earth. There is no record that they put gold on the inside of the tower. God confused the languages before the tower was finished, but without any record of fire. The tower of Babel was not the same as the pyramids of Egypt, though it might have been similar in shape.

THE TRUTH ABOUT HAGAR: Hagar's son was Ishmael, not Isaac, and they were wandering in the desert, not the jungle. They were going to die from thirst, not starvation, and thus, God provided water rather than food.

JUDGE DEBORAH PRESIDING: Unlike Demetrius's tale, Deborah was married to a man named Lappidoth. Deborah's palm was not outside of Ephesus but between Ramah and Bethel. The two women fighting over the baby were in King Solomon's court, not Deborah's. Deborah fought with Barak, not Cicero, but against Sisera. Deborah didn't say that people would make fun of Barak, but she said that he would not receive the honor for the victory. The song that Deborah and Barak sang is in the Book of Judges, not Psalms. We don't know how long Deborah lived or how she died. She was neither the last judge of Israel nor did she rule before Israel's first king, Saul, or Israel's second king, David.

ANYTHING FOR LOVE: Delilah lived in the Valley of Sorek, not Dagon. Samson attempted to throw Delilah off three times by lying about his strength. First, he said that he must be bound by seven fresh bowstrings, not yet dried. Then he said new ropes that had never been used would take all of his strength away. Finally, he said that seven locks of his hair must be woven into a loom. When Samson saw that Delilah would not give up on her quest, he told her the truth. Samson was not a Nazarene (someone from Nazareth), he was a Nazarite (someone who had taken a special religious vow). As a Nazarite, no razor had ever cut a hair on his head, rather than his beard, and his strength was in his hair.

MICAH'S IDOLS: There was a real man named Micah who spent eleven hundred pieces of silver to make some idols. He actually stole the money from his mother. When he returned the money, she suggested he use the coins to have some idols made. He did hire a priest, but one from Bethlehem. Scripture gives no indication that great crowds came or that the idols were given any name. Men from the tribe of Dan stole the idols, and they took the priest as well. When Micah went after them, though, he was not slaughtered. He simply realized he was outnumbered and turned back. The idols were set up in the house of God in Shiloh rather than the market-place in Dan. All of the rest is the result of the merchant's imagination.

FOR THE HAND OF THE KING'S DAUGHTER: The reason David didn't marry Saul's oldest daughter was because he felt unworthy to be Saul's son-in-law. And the king asked for the foreskins rather than the scalps of one hundred Philistines.

DAVID AND ABIGAIL: David saved Abigail from Nabal, not Nebel. Nabal offered David nothing—not even a slice of bread. Abigail is described as a beautiful woman, not an unattractive one. When Abigail approached David, she fell at his feet, but did not cover his feet with her hair. They were not interrupted by Nabal. It wasn't until the next day that Abigail told her husband what had happened. He instantly had a stroke and died ten days later. Nabal was not taken as a slave by David.

SONG OF A REPENTANT KING: King David wrote that he was sinful from his mother's womb and not that he learned to be sinful. He also wrote that ultimately his sin was only against God and no one else.

A HOUSE DIVIDED: Ahlil was right about many things, but it was the prophet Ahijah who talked to Jeroboam instead of Isaiah. Ahijah tore his own coat rather than Jeroboam's. Also, Ahijah tore the coat into twelve pieces to represent all the tribes of Israel. He gave Jeroboam ten of the pieces as an object lesson on how the kingdom would divide.

SENNACHERIB'S FALL: God sent an angel who killed Sennacherib's Assyrian army while they were still in their camp. When Sennacherib returned to his country he was killed as well.

HOW SICK IS HEZEKIAH?: Although Marta said at first that the king hadn't been sick, Hezekiah was actually at the point of death when Isaiah arrived. After Hezekiah prayed, Isaiah told him that his kingdom would be strong for fifteen more years, not the twenty years that Marta quoted. Isaiah healed the king with a poultice rather than by having him wash in the Jordan River. Hezekiah did ask for a sign, but the sign was that the sundial would move back ten intervals rather than forward.

ESTHER THE BRAVE: Esther actually worked within the traditions of her time. First, she didn't work her way into the king's palace. Instead, she was entered into a beauty contest and won the queenship. She didn't earn the right to speak to the king. No one earned that right. Instead, she threw herself at his mercy when she went to speak to him. Also, Rachel confused Mordecai and Haman. Mordecai was Esther's cousin. Haman was Mordecai's mortal enemy. Finally, the feast that Esther instituted, yet another tradition, was the Feast of Purim rather than the Feast of Booths. If anything, Esther saved her people by working within the traditions of the culture around her.

HOW THE WALL WAS WON: The wall actually did take only fifty-two days to complete. The workers, though, were anything but difficult. They worked hard and long to complete the wall in such a short time. They often had to hold a weapon in one hand and a tool in the other to protect their work and to keep the construction project going. Sanballet and Tobiah were the antagonists in the process rather than facilitators. The memo described a situation completely backward from the reality of Nehemiah's experience. Also, in the dedication Ezra only led part of the procession.

WILL THE REAL GOMER...: If it were Gomer, she didn't remember either the order or the names of her children. Her first child was Jezreel, named for the massacre that Jehu perpetrated. The second child was Lo-ruhamah, which meant "not loved," and the third child was Lo-ammi, which meant "not my people." The rest is true.

THE SOWER AND THE SEED: Where they actually became confused was on the very first seed. The seeds along the path were eaten by birds. They represent someone who doesn't understand the Word. The seeds on the rocky places were scorched because they had no roots. They represent someone who receives the Word but turns back because of difficulties. The seeds among the thorns were choked back by other plants. They represent the person who turns back because of the worries of life and the deceitfulness of wealth. The seeds on the good soil brought a good crop. They represent the person who hears the Word and understands it.

EQUAL PAY: The owner in the story was a landowner who ran a vineyard, not a winepress. The daily pay was one denarius (or a penny) rather than one dollar. The owner actually hired workers in the morning, the third hour, the sixth hour, the ninth hour, and the eleventh hour.

BEST SEATS IN THE HOUSE: Jesus said not to take the best seat because when someone more honored than you arrives, you'll be humiliated by being asked to move. He said instead to sit at the lowest place, and then you'll be honored when you're given a better seat.

THE FIRST CHRISTIAN MARTYR: It wasn't true that Stephen did not say a word. He preached an impassioned historical sermon beginning with Abraham, the father of the Jews. When Stephen was being stoned he did cry out as Jesus had from the cross, but instead of the quote Nola remembered, he instead commended his spirit to God and asked God to forgive his assailants. Saul of Tarsus, later Paul the apostle, was at the scene, but he was a persecutor rather than a defender. It was later that Paul became a believer.

A SISTER IN CHRIST: Lydia lived in Philippi rather than Pisidia. She would not have been anywhere near the Jordan River. It was Paul who baptized Lydia, not James or John. Paul did have companions with him, including Luke, but there's no record of James or John. Lydia was in a grasp of people praying, not meeting for Bible study. She did invite the apostles to stay at her home, but they did not live there. They only stayed until it was time to travel again.

WHO WAS APOLLOS?: There is more fiction in this account than truth. This is what is the Bible tells us: Apollos was a native of Alexandria; he was educated; he taught about Jesus accurately, but he only knew of the baptism of John; Priscilla and Aquila mentored him in the Christian faith; he became a great leader and influence in the early church.

HERO OR GOAT?: Paul's colleague was named Barnabas rather than Barsabas. Paul healed a man who was crippled, not one who was deaf. The crowd did call Paul Hermes (or Mercury), but they called Barnabas Zeus (or Jupiter). Paul and Barnabas did not take advantage of the crowd thinking they were gods. Instead, they tried to convince them otherwise. The men who persuaded the crowd against Paul were from Antioch and Iconium rather than Ephesus and Philippi.

SHIPWRECK ON MALTA: The ships that Paul was transferred to at Myra and Malta were of Alexandrian origin rather than Viking. When Paul prophesied to the sailors about the angel's message, the men actually believed him and were greatly encouraged. Publius's father was sick with fever and dysentery rather than leprosy. Paul and his shipmates spent three months on Malta (or Melita) as opposed to the twelve months listed here. Paul was relieved, rather than fearful, to find his friends in Puteoli. They took him to Rome, but they did not kidnap him.

UP ON THE ROOF: The home belonged to Simon the tanner rather than Simeon. Peter actually fell into a trance rather than dreamed in his sleep. The vision was of a sheet with unclean animals on it, not a magic carpet with a pig. The sheet appeared three times rather than four. There were three men, and not two, who came from Cornelius's house. Also, Cornelius lived in Caesarea rather than Joppa.

HIGH PROFILE PRISONER MISSING: It was Herod rather than Pilate who imprisoned Peter. Herod had James killed before Peter was imprisoned. The angel didn't fly Peter over the city. Instead, he left Peter just inside the gate, and Peter found his way to Mary's house. The part about Rhoda leaving Peter at the door was entirely true.

LIKE JOKES OR TRIVIA?

Then check out these great books from
Barbour Publishing!